The Jewish Genealogical So
Registered Charity N

A Guide to Jewish Genealogy in Germany & Austria

No. 2 in the series

Edited by:

Thea Skyte
Member of the JGSGB German SIG

Randol Schoenberg
Member of the JewishGen Bohemia-Moravia SIG

Rosemary Wenzerul
Chairman
JGSGB Education Committee

זכר ימות עולם בינו שנות דר-ודר
שאל אביך ויגדך זקניך ויאמרו-לך :
Remember the days of old; consider the years of many generations:
Ask thy father, and he will declare unto thee: Thine elders, and they will tell thee.
Deuteronomy XXX11 v.7   דברים לב ז

Published by
The Jewish Genealogical Society of Great Britain
Registered Charity No. 1022738
PO Box 13288, London, N3 3WD.
E-mail: jgsgb@ort.org
Web site: www.jgsgb.ort.org

Printed by
The Printing Place Ltd
☎ 01245 251001

ISBN 0-9537669-1-8

Front cover designed by
Rosemary Hoffman and Derek Wenzerul

CONTENTS

PART II - AUSTRIA

PART III - GENERAL INFORMATION

FOREWORD

'A Guide to Jewish Genealogy in Germany & Austria' is the second publication in the 'Jewish Ancestors' series of booklets to be produced by The Jewish Genealogical Society of Great Britain. It will enable our members and others who are researching their German/Austrian ancestors to be pointed in the right direction by covering as many areas of research as possible both in the UK and abroad. We have split the guide into three parts, namely Germany, Austria and General Information. In doing so, we have unavoidably had to repeat some of the information but have tried, where possible, to cross-reference the sections. Maps have been provided to show the various boundary changes.

Genealogy is a very popular and fast growing interest. Whilst increased accessibility to both computers and the Internet have made many more resources available to everyone, there is still no substitute for visiting archives and looking at records.

We hope this Guide will give an insight into the world of Jewish genealogy in Germany and Austria and encourage further research in the future.

I would like to take the opportunity of thanking the following members of the Education Committee and the Society for their help in producing the Guide:

Ken Ambrose, Margaret Arenias, Jonathan Borchard, Dr. Cyril Fox, Peter Glass, Maurice Hoffman, Rosemary Hoffman, Dr. Saul Issroff, Peter Landé, Jeanette Rosenberg, Randol Schoenberg, Jürgen Sielemann, Heinz and Thea Skyte. In addition, I am indebted to David Fielker for his editorial advice, John Levy for his extremely meticulous proof reading, Derek Wenzerul for all his help with the technical side of producing the Guide and to all the organisations and archives in the UK, Germany and Austria who very kindly supplied us with so much information.

I must mention that 85% of the information on Germany was supplied and written by Thea and Heinz Skyte whose commitment and enthusiasm has enabled the guide to be produced so quickly. Thea and Heinz are members of the Society's German Special Interest Group (SIG) and we are very grateful to them for all their effort. In addition, Randol Schoenberg, who is a Member of JewishGen's Bohemia-Moravia SIG, wrote all of the Austrian section. We are very grateful to him also for all his help.

Rosemary Wenzerul
Chairman, JGSGB Education Committee
Member of Council

January 2001

INTRODUCTION

For centuries, Jews in Germany and Austria were persecuted, oppressed and, in certain areas, forced to live in ghettos like Jews elsewhere in continental Europe.

During the first half of the 19th century, following the French Revolution and the 'Enlightenment', Jews in Western Europe were gradually emancipated. The second half of the 19th and the first three decades of the 20th century was a time of extraordinary cultural, scientific and economic achievement for German and Austrian Jews. Then came persecution more terrible than anything the Jews had yet experienced, and the almost complete destruction of Jewish life in this area.

A substantial number of German and Austrian Jews managed to escape before it was too late; most of them emigrated to the USA or Palestine. About 50,000 Jewish refugees came to Britain (most of them settling in north-west London), where they joined Jews from Poland, Russia and other eastern European countries who had arrived here some 50 years earlier.

After the Second World War, few Jewish refugees returned to Germany and Austria. The Jewish communities in those countries today are a shadow of their former selves.

Yet a surprisingly large quantity of German-Jewish records survived the Holocaust, and there is much for genealogists to discover about their ancestors.

John Levy
Member, JGSGB
German Special Interest Group

January 2001

6

PART I
GERMANY

BORDERS

Germany's borders have changed several times over the last 130 years. Before 1871 Germany consisted of some independent kingdoms, grand duchies, duchies and many small independent territories. In 1871 the Kingdom of Prussia, later to become a state, extended much further east, taking in the Prussian province of Posen (Poznan), as well as the Memelland, the most northerly part of what was then East Prussia, which in 1923 became part of Lithuania.

In 1918, after the First World War, Posen (Poznan) became part of Poland and East Prussia was separated from the rest of Germany by the so-called 'Polish Corridor'. In 1945 after the end of the Second World War all territory east of the river Oder became part of Poland and East Prussia was ceded to Russia. The remaining parts of Germany were divided into the Federal Republic of Germany (West Germany) and the German Democratic Republic (East Germany). Berlin, at this time situated in the middle of East Germany, also became a divided city - West Berlin under the control of the Western Allies, and East Berlin under the control of the Soviet Union. In 1961 the infamous Berlin Wall physically separated the city. East and West Germany and of course Berlin were eventually re-united in 1990.

German states and provinces differ between the various periods and the present time. Some knowledge of these may help in finding records.

**PLEASE NOTE THAT NONE OF THE MAPS
IN THE GUIDE ARE DRAWN TO SCALE**

Map showing Germany's changing borders from 1871 to after 1945

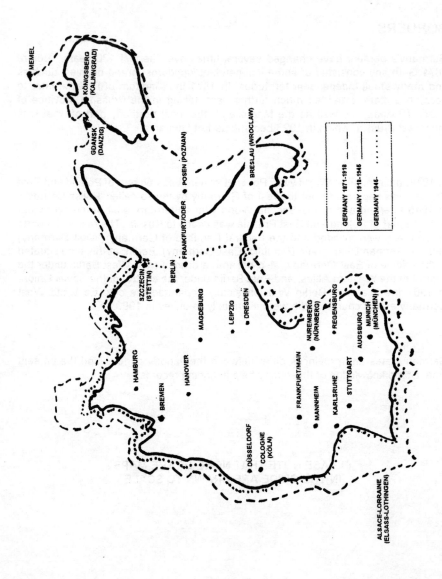

Legend:

GERMANY 1871-1918 – – –
GERMANY 1918-1945 ———
GERMANY 1945- · · · · · ·

Labels: MEMEL, KÖNIGSBERG (KALININGRAD), GDANSK (DANZIG), POSEN (POZNAN), FRANKFURT/ODER, BRESLAU (WROCLAW), SZCZECIN (STETTIN), BERLIN, MAGDEBURG, LEIPZIG, DRESDEN, NUREMBERG (NÜRNBERG), REGENSBURG, AUGSBURG, MUNICH (MÜNCHEN), HAMBURG, BREMEN, HANOVER, FRANKFURT/MAIN, MANNHEIM, KARLSRUHE, STUTTGART, DÜSSELDORF, COLOGNE (KÖLN), ALSACE-LORRAINE (ELSASS-LOTHINGEN)

Between 1918 and 1945

Germany was divided into 'Staaten' (states) as below.
Prussia, formerly the largest of these, no longer existed. It included the provinces of Brandenburg, Grenzmark Posen-Westpreussen (now part of Poland), Hannover (Hanover), Hessen-Nassau, Ostpreussen (East Prussia, now part of Russia), Provinz Sachsen (Province of Saxony), Rhein Provinz (Rhineland), Schlesien (Silesia, now part of Poland), Schleswig-Holstein and Westphalen (Westphalia).

The other 'Staaten' were:
Baden, Bayern (Bavaria) including the Province Pfalz (Palatinate), Hessen (Hesse), Mecklenburg, Oldenburg, Thüringen (Thuringia), Württemberg, as well as the 'Freistaaten' (republics) of Anhalt, Bremen, Hamburg and Lübeck.

GERMANY AND GERMAN STATES AT THE PRESENT TIME

- - - Border 1945-1990 between:
Federal Republic of Germany (West Germany)
and
German Democratic Republic of Germany (East Germany)

——— Berlin was also a divided city 1945-1990 (East and West Berlin)

Post 1945

After 1945 Germany was divided into 'Länder' (states). The present states and administrative districts are: Baden-Württemberg, Bayern (Bavaria), Berlin, Brandenburg, Bremen, Hamburg, Hessen (Hesse), Mecklenburg-Vorpommern (Mecklenburg-West Pomerania), Niedersachsen (Lower Saxony), Nordrhein-Westfalen (North Rhine-Westphalia), Rheinland-Pfalz (Rhineland-Palatinate), Saarland, Sachsen (Saxony), Sachsen-Anhalt, Schleswig-Holstein, Thüringen (Thuringia). (See pages 28-30 for a list of Landes- and Staatsarchiv (State archives) and page 42 for Internet addresses)

Names of Towns
Most German and English names of towns are the same or very similar. There are a few exceptions.

GERMAN	ENGLISH
Köln	Cologne
München	Munich

Breslau, formerly in Silesia, Germany, and since 1945 in Poland, is now Wrocław.

There are two cities in Germany called Frankfurt: Frankfurt am Main (west) and Frankfurt an der Oder (east).

Frankfurt/Oder
The river Oder divides Frankfurt and since 1945 is also the German/Polish frontier. The part west of the river is German and known as Frankfurt, whereas the part east of the Oder is called Stubice.

Stettin, although divided by the river Oder, is now in Poland (Szczecin).

Königsberg, formerly in East Prussia and since 1945 part of Russia, is now Kaliningrad.

STARTING YOUR RESEARCH

WHERE TO START

Before embarking on actual research, try to gather as much information as possible on your family from relatives and friends.

INFORMATION AVAILABLE IN THE UK

WIENER LIBRARY

4 Devonshire Street, London, W1N 2BH
Tel: 020 7636 7247 - Fax: 020 7436 6428
E-mail: lib@wl.u-net.com
The library is an invaluable source of information on German Jewry, the Nazi period, the Holocaust and anti-Semitism. Apart from its books on German subjects and towns, the library has some published and unpublished family histories and trees. It also has memorial books for a number of towns, and those issued in 1986 by the German Government with names of Jews who met their death in the various concentration camps (the latter does not cover the former East Germany). There are photographic and press archives. The Wiener Library does not undertake research and is primarily a Holocaust archive and library. (See section on the Holocaust for further information and additional places in the UK, which hold yizkor books.)

LDS FAMILY HISTORY CENTRE - MORMONS

The Mormons have the largest collection of genealogical records in the world, including many Jewish records. There are Family History Centres in most major cities and towns in Great Britain (for a full list see the publication *'Jewish Ancestors? A Beginner's Guide to Jewish Genealogy in Great Britain'* - details on page 76) or look at their web site on http://www.familysearch.org/search. The address of the London centre is: The Hyde Park Family History Centre, Church of Jesus Christ of the Latter Day Saints, 64-68 Exhibition Road, South Kensington, London, SW7 2PA. Tel: 020 7589 8561. It is closed all day Sunday and Monday.

The Mormons have German and Austrian Jewish records on microfilm, from the late 18th to the early 20th century. Each Family History Centre has a computerised index to the microfilms, many of which have to be ordered from the USA. There is a charge for each reservation, and it takes about a month for the films to arrive. Photocopies can be made from the microfilms for a nominal charge. Apart from this, there is no charge for using the facilities at the Centre.

To find information type 'Germany, the province, town' and 'Jewish records'.

(See page 48 for further details.)

PUBLIC RECORD OFFICE

Ruskin Avenue, Kew, Richmond, Surrey. TW9 4DU.
Tel: 020 8876 3444 - Fax: 020 8878 8905
Web site: http://www.pro.gov.uk
The Public Record Office holds documents on *immigration, information on denizations and naturalizations, Home Office indexes, copies and some details of naturalization certificates. Indexes of birth, marriage and death registers are available from the 17th century until 1837 (from 1837 onwards they are available at the Family Record Centre). In addition, there are census returns and internment records from World War I and II. (*See article by Petra Laidlaw in the December 2000 edition of Shemot, Vol.8 No.4.)

ALIEN REGISTRATION

Alien Registration in Great Britain was introduced as a way of keeping track of those individuals of foreign birth who had not been naturalized. The individuals were given alien registration certificates, which were internal passports. These had to be stamped by the local constabulary whenever the alien changed jobs, place of residence or travelled to another locality. The legislation passed in 1914, included provisions for alien restriction and internment. Many alien records in Great Britain have been destroyed. However, the Public Record Office and Home Office hold most of the records although some documentation may be found in local Police Stations, Police or District Archives. There is a book on this topic entitled 'The Internment of Aliens in Twentieth Century Britain' edited by David Cesarani and Tony Kushner. Further information may be found in JewishGen Archives.

FAMILY RECORD CENTRE

1 Myddelton Street, London, EC1R 1UW.
Tel: 020 8392 5300 - Fax: 020 8392 5307
Web site: http://www.open.gov.uk/pro/prohome.htm
The Centre holds birth, marriage and death records for England and Wales from 1837 onwards (from the 17th Century until 1837 they are held at the Public Record Office, Kew). You can order copies of the certificates for a relatively small fee, which will be forwarded by post within about a week.

PROBATE SEARCH ROOMS

Principal Registry of the Family Division,
First Avenue House, 42-49 High Holborn, London, WC1V 6NP.
Tel: 020 7936 6000 and 020 7936 6801
(Records previously held at Somerset House)
Some useful information may be found in copies of wills for England and Wales since 1858.

THE BRITISH LIBRARY - NEWSPAPER LIBRARY

Colindale Avenue, London, NW9 5HE.
Tel: 020 7412 7353 - Fax: 020 7412 7379
The library holds a number of German and Austrian newspapers, but unfortunately they do not have copies of the newspapers Neues Wiener Abendblatt or Jüdische Rundschau. However, they do have copies of: Aufbau 1943-1945 (American/German) - also available on web site: http://www.aufbau2000.com;

Berliner Tageblatt 1895-1939 (Shelf Ref: MF377) - this was a very popular daily Berlin newspaper; and the Neue Freie Presse 1885-January 1939. Another newspaper of interest is the Jüdisches Gemeindeblatt. The Neues Wiener Abendblatt and Neue Freie Presse newspapers are mentioned in the Austrian section of this guide as being the two papers in which Jewish families always put death notices. (For further details see Austrian National Library on page 51.)

MAP RESOURCES FOR GERMAN TOWNS
Royal Geographical Society
Map Room, Kensington Gore, London, SW7 2AR.
Tel: 020 7591 3040 - Fax: 020 7591 3001
E-mail: library@rgs.org
The Royal Geographical Society has over 900,000 maps, the largest collection in the world. These include early 19th-century maps of Germany before the Prussian-led unification, which clearly showed the boundaries of the network of small principalities and enclaves, useful for determining where personal documents are likely to have been located, as the boundaries seemed to change each decade. If you are planning a visit it is advisable to notify in advance the places you wish to find, with alternative spellings, and the date and scale of the maps required. (See article by George Rigal in the June 1998 edition of *Shemot,* Vol.6, No.2.)

EXTENDING YOUR SEARCH TO GERMANY
Vital Records (Registration of births, marriages and deaths)
Civil registration of births, marriages and deaths in German States was introduced from 1790 onwards varying from state to state. In Bavaria, for instance, a law was passed in 1813 ordering separate registers of all Jewish births, marriages and deaths. The clergy of the local Protestant or Catholic churches of the particular town or village usually kept these. Many of these registers are still in existence; some are still held by the churches, others can be found in the appropriate state archives of the area. No importance in early German records should be given to different spellings of locations, family names or varying first names.

A law for civil registration of all births, marriages and deaths, irrespective of faith, was passed on 6 February 1875 and came into force on 1 January 1876, when registry offices in Germany started.

In 1938/39 a law was passed forcing all Jews to register the additional Jewish first names of Israel for a man or Sara for a woman as from 1 January 1939 and additional entries of these were made in the birth registers. For genealogical purposes these forced additional first names should be disregarded.

There is no central registry office for the whole of Germany: each town keeps its own records. Pre-1876 German civil registration records that have survived are generally deposited in the respective state archives, whereas post-1876 records are kept in the respective 'Standesämter' (registry offices).

Copies of certificates for more recent years and/or not relating to direct ancestors may be difficult to obtain because of the German law governing access to the registers of births, marriages and deaths (Personenstandsgesetz). Normally laws regulating the use of archives in Germany allow the use of records 110 years after a person's birth, 90 years after a person's marriage and 30 years after a person's death. This does not apply in the case of the civil registration offices, the (Standesämter). Information from all their records can only be obtained by descendants or in the case of legal interest. When writing to a German Standesämt always ask for a photocopy of the original entry, otherwise you may only receive an extract which does not contain all the data of the original entry.

Fig. 1 - Part of Family Record Book

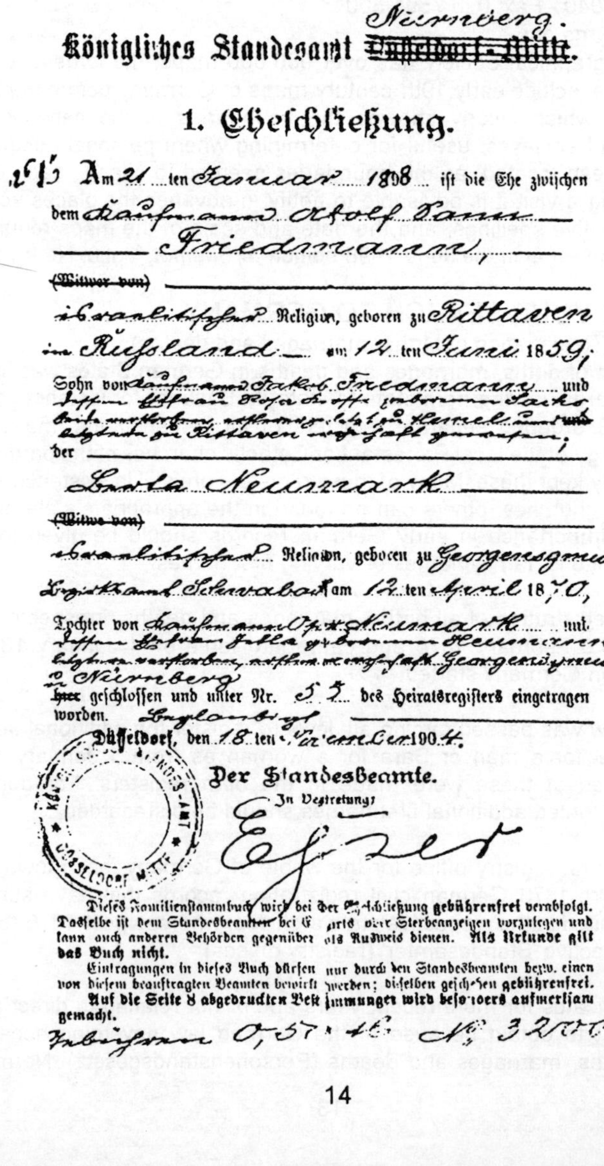

Nürnberg.

Königliches Standesamt ~~Düsseldorf - Mitte.~~

1. Eheschließung.

Am 21 ten Januar 1808 ist die Ehe zwischen dem Kaufmann Adolf Samuel Friedmann, _(Wittwer von)_

israelitischer Religion, geboren zu Rittaven in Rußland am 12 ten Juni 1859, Sohn von Kaufmann Jakob Friedmann und dessen Ehefrau Rosa Friedmann geborenen Jacks beide verstorben, zuletzt wohnhaft... zuletzt in Rittaven ... der

Berta Neumark _(Wittwe von)_

israelitischer Religion, geboren zu Georgensgmünd Bezirksamt Schwabach am 12 ten April 1870, Tochter von Kaufmann Opel Neumark und dessen Ehefrau Jetta geborenen Heumann beide verstorben, zuletzt wohnhaft Georgensgmünd & Nürnberg hier geschlossen und unter Nr. 55 des Heiratsregisters eingetragen worden. England...

Düsseldorf, den 18 ten Dezember 1904.

Der Standesbeamte.

In Vertretung,

Esser

Dieses Familienstammbuch wird bei der Eheschließung gebührenfrei verabfolgt. Dasselbe ist dem Standesbeamten bei Geburts oder Sterbeanzeigen vorzulegen und kann auch anderen Behörden gegenüber als Ausweis dienen. Als Urkunde gilt das Buch nicht.

Eintragungen in dieses Buch dürfen nur durch den Standesbeamten bezw. einen von diesem beauftragten Beamten bewirkt werden; dieselben geschehen gebührenfrei. Auf die Seite 8 abgedruckten Bestimmungen wird besonders aufmerksam gemacht.

14

Fig. 2 - Part of Family Record Book

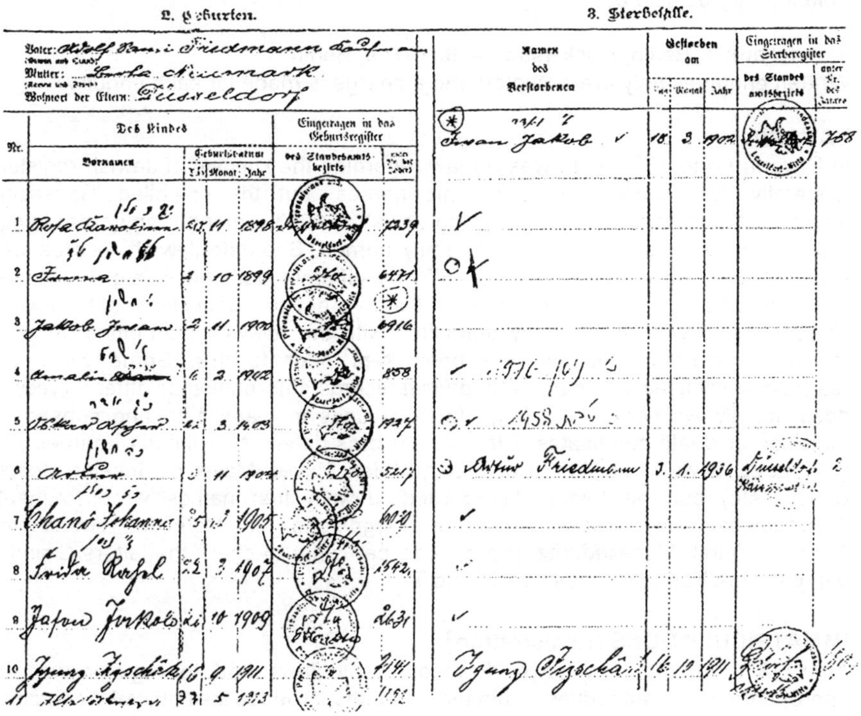

FAMILY RECORD BOOK (See examples on pages 14-15 - Figs. 1 and 2)
The Family Record book was provided free of charge at the wedding. It had to be presented to the registrar at notifications of births and deaths and could also be used before other authorities as proof of identity. It was not valid as a legal document. Entries into this book could only be made by the registrar or his deputy and were free of charge.

BERLIN
There is no central office for the whole of Berlin, but there are more than 20 of these, each district having its own. Some of these are being amalgamated. If the exact address and the district are not known, the following may be of use. Write to the address below, giving first and family names of a person and exact date or a time span of not more than four years:

Senatsverwaltung fur Inneres in Berlin
IC 506/507, Fehrbelliner Platz 1, D-10702, Berlin.
There is a charge for each enquiry, which may take several months.

FOR FORMER EAST GERMANY AND FORMER GERMAN TERRITORIES

Any surviving registration records of Jews who lived in the former East Germany and in former German territories (Danzig, Posen/Poznan, Silesia) which are now in Poland, may be held by:

Standesamt 1, Berlin, Rückerstrasse 9, 10119, Berlin
Written enquiries only are accepted and a charge is made for each enquiry.

BAVARIA

In Bavaria up to 1807 there was no law regarding the keeping of Jewish registers. Generally Jews only had patronymic names, but the so-called 'Bayerische Judenedict' (Bavarian Edict concerning Jews) of 1813, among many other things, ordered all Jews to adopt German family names. Separate Jewish records were kept between the early 1800s and 1876 by different authorities, e.g. the Jewish community itself, but mostly by the local Catholic or Protestant clergy of the town or village. These were periodically deposited with the relevant authorities. In some towns, registers in Hebrew had been kept prior to this. Some were later retrospectively used as the basis for official records. Information on different records does not always correspond (e.g. dates or ages on early birth and subsequent marriage or death certificates). In early records different spellings of names (e.g. Levi, Levy, Lewi, Levin, Lewin or Meier, Maier, Meyer, Mayer or Scheidt, Scheid, Scheit, etc) can be totally disregarded. Jewish first names were frequently 'Germanised' e.g. Madel becoming Magdalene or Mathilde, Aron/Anton, Abraham/Adolf, Moses/Moritz. It may also be useful to check the letters C and K, e.g. Caroline/Karoline, as well as D and T.

IMMATRICULATIONS (Registration)

After 1813 (1816/17 in Lower Franconia) all Jews had to register with the appropriate police authorities within three months, produce their official 'Schutzbrief' (Letter of Protection) and licences of their Grant of Domicile, giving details of their position, age, numbers in their families and their means of livelihood. Those who had not previously had family names, which was mostly the case, were asked to state the family name they would adopt. They were not allowed to choose names of well-known families or those already in common use.

All details were entered in lists, the 'Juden Matrikel' (Registration of Jews), and each was given a 'Matrikel' number - 'Immatrikuliering'. For Jews to be able to settle, work and marry in a particular place they were required to apply for 'Matrikel'. Jews were only allowed to live in places where Jewish communities had existed prior to the edict and their numbers were to be strictly limited, could not be increased and, if at all possible, should be reduced.

Only the 'Emanzipationsedikt' (Emancipation Law) of 10 November 1861 finally gave Jews full equality, did away with 'Matrikel' laws and allowed Jews to settle anywhere in Bavaria. This led to the movement of many Jews from villages where they had lived for some centuries into towns. Many 'Matrikel' lists have survived and are deposited in various local or state archives.

BAVARIA

EINWOHNERMELDEAMT (Registration Office)

In Germany people have to register their addresses and change of address with their respective local offices. Access to these is restricted for varying periods in different towns. Older records are usually transferred to respective archives of the town. These are particularly useful, as they often give very detailed information of members of the particular family, their names, occupation, address and dates of birth, marriage and death - with names of spouses.

RECORDS FOR THE FORMER PRUSSIAN PROVINCE OF POSEN

GERMANY
Stiftung 'Neue Synagoge Berlin - Centrum Judaicum'
Oranienburgerstrasse 28/30, D-10117, Berlin.
Some records of the former Prussian Province of Posen (Poznan) are held.
(See page 28 for further details)

ISRAEL
Central Archives for the History of the Jewish People
Sprinzak Building, Hebrew University, Givat Ram, Jerusalem.
(See page 32 for further details.)

POLAND
Archiwum Panstwowe Usc
ul. 23 Lutego 41/43, 60-967 Posen, Poland.
Records (over 100 years old) are held for some Jewish communities of the former Province Posen (Poznan) since 1919.

Jewish Historical Institute of Poland
ul. Tlomackie 3/5, 00-090 Warsaw, Poland.
Remnants of some Jewish Communal archives of Province Posen (Poznan) communities 1700-1938 are held.
The above Institute also holds Jewish records for:
Breslau (Wroclaw) from its inception until World War II; Bromberg (Brydgoszcz) district collection 1838-1938; Schlesien (Silesia) records for many Jewish communities mainly covering the years 1742-1942; Various records are held from Bialystok, Litzmannstadt and Warsaw Ghettos, from 1939-1945.

CENSUSES
Until 1871 there were no censuses covering the entire German Empire. The 1819 census for the Grand Duchy of Mecklenburg-Schwerin includes the following: name, date and place of birth, sex, religion, spouse's name and occupation, how long they had been living in the community, where and when the spouse was born and the length of time they had been resident in the community.

1933 Census
Jews in Germany according to the census of 1933:

German states and provinces differ between then and the present time. Preussen (Prussia), formerly the largest German state, which included the provinces of Berlin, Brandenburg, Hanover, Hessen-Nassau, Ostpreussen (East Prussia), Rheinland (Rhineland), Sachsen (Saxony), Schlesien (Silesia, now part of Poland), Schleswig-Holstein and Westfalen (Westphalia), no longer exists.

STATE	NO. OF JEWS	STATE	NO. OF JEWS
Prussia	361,826	Saxony	20,584
Baden	20,617	Other States	54,716
Bavaria	41,939		

1939 Census
This census was taken in May 1939 in all regions of Germany including the former Sudetenland, which had been annexed from Czechoslovakia. Records for Thuringia and a few towns in the Rhineland have been lost.

Census returns from so-called 'non-Aryans' were extracted to identify people with Jewish origins and list all members of the family at the address, their first names (the additional names of Sara and Israel, which German Jews had to adopt from the 1 January 1939 should be disregarded), family and maiden names, dates and places of birth, details of education as well as family members temporarily away from home. An additional question to be answered was 'Is or was one of your four grandparents according to race 'Volljude'? (A Jewish person with four Jewish grandparents.) This had to be answered with 'yes' or 'no' separately for each of the four.

Church of Jesus Christ of the Latter Day Saints or 'LDS' (Mormons)
Microfilms of the 1939 census can be ordered at LDS Family History Centres. It is catalogued under 'Germany', 'State', 'Town' (for larger towns, e.g. Berlin, then alphabetically by name) and 'Jewish records'. (See entries on pages 11 and 48.)

EMIGRATION
Although Jews in the various German states gradually became German citizens during the 19th century and unlike their brethren in Eastern Europe did not suffer terrible pogroms, there was a lot of anti-Semitism and different laws came into force restricting their movement, their education and economic, commercial and professional progress. This led quite a number of Jews to emigrate from around the middle of the 19th century onwards to try and find a brighter future, mainly in Great Britain and the United States.

In the 1930s, owing to Nazi oppression and tyranny, it became obvious that emigration was becoming vital. Individual Jews as well as whole Jewish families tried desperately to find a country where they would be safe. In the early 1930s many fled to Belgium, France or the Netherlands only to find themselves once again in the same situation. Emigration became more difficult as time went on, particularly for those individuals who were less well off or had no relatives abroad. People had to provide proof that they would not become a financial burden on the country giving them refuge. To immigrate to the United States an affidavit, a sponsorship, by an American citizen was required. Even if such a document was in hand the annual quota allowed to enter was strictly limited, building up a waiting list in the late 1930s of some three to four years. In Great Britain there were also restrictions. People had to prove that they had financial security and safe jobs to go to, some of which had age restrictions. Jews also tried to immigrate to Australia, New Zealand, Palestine, South Africa, South American countries of Argentina, Brazil, Chile, Uruguay etc or any country that would accept them.
Shanghai. In the late 1930s a substantial number of German and Austrian Jews managed to emmigrate to Shanghai. An 'Emigranten Adressbuch fuer Shanghai mit Branchen-Register' New Star Company, Shanghai, 1939, re-printed Old China Press, Hong Kong, 1995 lists their Shanghai address and also their towns of origin and profession. Names of refugees who died in Shanghai were also recorded. Copies of both the address book and the death lists can be found at the Leo Baeck Institute in New York (see page 31) and also in the US Holocaust Memorial Museum in Washington (see page 23).

Hidden Persons

In Belgium, France and Holland, some people were saved by being hidden by families and institutions, e.g. monasteries. Some of these subsequently adopted the religion of their protectors.

Kindertransport

After 9/10 November 1938, the so called 'Kristallnacht', the refugee issue was debated by the British Government, which on the 21 November 1938 announced that it would allow a number of children under the age of 17 years to enter Britain for each of whom a security bond of £50 was required. Jewish and non-Jewish organisations, commercial firms and individuals got together to try to raise money and gifts. Stanley Baldwin, a former British Prime Minister, made a radio appeal. This resulted in the setting up of the 'Kindertransporte', children's transports, the first of these transports arriving in England on 2 December 1938. Between then and the outbreak of war, some 10,000 unaccompanied children from Nazi-occupied countries, varying in age from babies to those under the age of 17, entered Britain. Most but not all of them were Jewish. They were either cared for by relatives, individual families and organisations or accommodated in various hostels throughout Great Britain. Most of the children never saw their parents again.

UK Address:

Kindertransport Association,
c/o Association of Jewish Refugees in Great Britain (AJR)
1 Hampstead Gate, 1a Frognal, London, NW3 6AL.
Tel/Fax: 020 7431 1821

The Kindertransport Association does not hold records or provide facilities for research. However, World Jewish Relief holds over 400,000 records of refugees. These are not open to the public for research purposes but on written application, information will be supplied.

Apply to:
World Jewish Relief
The Forum, 74 Camden Street, London, NW1 OEG.
Tel: 020 7691 1774 - Fax: 020 7691 1780

HOLOCAUST

The Holocaust is a very specialised subject. We hope therefore that the following will give you an insight into where to obtain information.

CONCENTRATION CAMPS, KILLING CENTRES AND GHETTOS

Soon after the Nazis came into power in 1933 concentration camps were set up. The main ones then were Buchenwald, Dachau, Florrenburg, Ravensbrück (for women) and Sachsenhausen in Germany, and Mauthausen in Austria. During World War II they increased in size and numbers, the best-known ones being Auschwitz, Belzec, Bergen Belsen, Gross Rosen, Izbica, Kulmhof (Chelmno), Lodz, Maidanek, Minsk, Riga, Sobibor, Stutthof, Theresienstadt and Treblinka.

Holocaust web site: www.JewishGen.org\ForgottenCamps.

WHERE TO START FINDING A MISSING RELATIVE
BELIEVED TO BE A VICTIM OF THE HOLOCAUST

1939 CENSUS

Lists are catalogued by the name of the town and may therefore be of little use, unless the town where the person lived at that time is known. Some named individuals may still have been able to emigrate after the census was taken in May 1939. (See pages 18 and 19 for further details.)

DEPORTATION LISTS

Some German towns have published lists of people deported from their town. It should however be borne in mind that some people may have been forced to move from their normal place of residence before being deported. Yad Vashem, Jerusalem, Israel, (see page 23) also holds some of these lists.

MEMORIAL BOOKS

The German Government in 1986 issued 'Gedenkbuch: Opfer der Verfolgung der deutschen Juden', a memorial book in two volumes, which however only covered the former West Germany. The volumes include the names of about 125,000 'German' Jews. These were not limited by citizenship or birth but rather included all Jews resident in Germany who were murdered. They are arranged in alphabetical order of surname, giving date of birth etc. Where the place of death is not known the word 'Verschollen' (missing) is written, i.e. the individual was deported but nothing further is known. 'Für tot Erklärt' - means declared dead by a German Court. When newer sources of information and the former Eastern Germany are included it is expected that the number of names will rise to about 200,000. (Jews from other countries, e.g. Hungary or Poland, who were shipped to Germany for forced labour and then were murdered or died there were not included in the old Gedenkbuch and will not be included in the new one.)

Apart from the above, many towns and some states also have published their own memorial books. Amongst these are - Berlin, Cologne (Köln), Frankfurt/Main, Fürth,

Hamburg, Hanover, Leipzig and Nuremberg (Nürnberg) . Books for other towns are constantly being prepared. They are too numerous to mention, as many need updating, owing to new data continually becoming available. While some of these books only give the name, date of birth and date and place of death (if known), others give details of the individuals, names of their parents, spouses and siblings and other information, some also including photographs. Several lists can be searched on the Internet.

Some Memorial Books and other Holocaust related material may be found at:

Wiener Library
4 Devonshire Street, London, W1N 2BH.
Tel: 020 7636 7247 - Fax: 020 7436 6428
E-mail: lib@wl.u-net.com (See Page 11 for further details.)
(See JGSGB Journal, Shemot, December 1999, Vol.7, No.4, pages 23-25, which gives a summary of the books held in the Wiener Library. These were mainly on the fate of communities, often with lists of names. (Copies of Shemot are held in the JGSGB Library.)

The following libraries have collections:

The British Library, Oriental & India Office Collections	96 Euston Road, London, NW1 2DB. Tel: 020 7412 7332 - Fax: 020 7412 7858
Cambridge University Library	West Road, Cambridge, CB3 9DR. Tel: 01223 333 000 - Fax: 01223 333 160
The Jewish Genealogical Society of Great Britain (JGSGB)	See page 37 for details
Leopold Muller Memorial Library	Oxford Centre for Hebrew & Jewish Studies, Yarnton Manor, Yarnton, Oxfordshire. OX5 1PY. Tel: 01865 375079 (by appointment)
London School of Jewish Studies (formerly Jews' College)	See page 33 for details
Hartley Library	University of Southampton, Highfield, Southampton, SO17 1BJ. Tel: 023 8059 2180 - Fax: 023 8059 5451 E-mail: library@soton.ac.uk
School of Oriental & African Studies (SOAS)	University of London, Thornhaugh Street, Russell Square, London, WC1H OXG. Charge for browsing - £6 per day Tel: 020 7898 4163 - Fax: 020 7898 4159
University College, London	Gower Street, London, WC1E 6BT. Tel: 020 7387 7050 - Fax: 020 7380 7373
Wiener Library (Institute of Contemporary History)	4 Devonshire Street, London, W1N 2BH. Tel: 020 7636 7247 - Fax: 020 7436 6428 E-mail: lib@wl.u-net.com

A list of yizkor books, shtetl by shtetl alphabetically, has been compiled by Zachary Baker and can be found in Arthur Kurzweil's book, 'From Generation to Generation', Harper-Perennial, 1994. (Can be found in the JGSGB library.)

WHERE TO FIND FURTHER INFORMATION

The primary sources for Holocaust research are:
Yad Vashem Martyrs' and Heroes Remembrance Authority (Hall of Names)
PO Box 3477, 91034 Jerusalem, Israel.
Web site: http://www.yadvashem.org.il
Yad Vashem recently opened a new combined library and archive. Owing to limited staffing, research may have to be done personally. Having said this, the Hall of Names will respond to personal inquiries for research purposes. Yad Vashem is also in the process of computerising its lists, which in due course will be published on the Internet.

United States Holocaust Memorial Museum
100 Raoul Wallenberg Place, SW, Washington, DC 20024-2150, USA.
E-mail: research@ushmm.org
Web site: http://www.ushmm.org
The United States Holocaust Research Institute houses a Holocaust library and archive as well as photograph and oral history archives. It has records of most of the concentration camps, killing centres and ghettos. It also has the 'Registry of Jewish Holocaust Survivors' now known as the 'Names Registry'.
E-mail: registry@ushmm.org.

Holocaust Education Trust
BCM Box 7892, London, WC1N 3XX.
Tel: 020 7222 6822 - Fax: 020 7233 0161
E-mail: hetrust@compuserve.com
Web site: http://www.het.org.uk

The House of the Wannsee Conference
Am Grossen Wannsee 56-58, D-14109 Berlin
Tel: +49 30 80 50 01 - 0   Fax: +49 30 80 50 01 27
E-mail: library@ghwk.de
Web site: www.ghwk.de
The Wannsee Villa contains an exhibition showing the entire process of the Holocaust, from segregation and persecution to the deportation and eventual murder of the Jews of Germany and all the lands the Third Reich conquered. There is a very good library that has a wealth of material including registers with names. They will respond to written requests. There is an excellent booklet available at a low price describing the exhibition.

Search Bureau for Missing Persons
HaSochnut HaYehudi, PO Box 92, Jerusalem, Israel.
Tel: +972 2 6202652 - Fax: +972 2 6202893

International Tracing Service - British Red Cross
British Red Cross, International Welfare Department, 9 Grosvenor Crescent, London, SW1X 7EJ. Tel: 020 7235 5454
The British Red Cross in Arolsen, Germany hold records of civilians who suffered in the Holocaust and details of concentration camps. Enquiries take a considerable

time and should be sent initially to the address in the UK, which is shown on the previous page.

Auschwitz	Most of the original death books were destroyed. Remaining death books from Auschwitz were published in three volumes in 1995 by: Auschwitz Museum, POB 32-603, Oswiecim 5, Poland. Death books for Auschwitz Remnants Ed. J. Debski 1995. A limited number of records have been computerised by the United States Holocaust Memorial Museum. For details see: http://www.ushmm.org.
Belzec	Was originally set up as a forced labour camp but became a death camp in 1942, when 550,000 Jews were killed there between March and December of that year. There are no lists.
Bergen Belsen	Prisoners from all over Europe. A 'Gedenkbuch Häftlinge des Konzentrationslager Bergen Belsen' (Memorial book of prisoners of the Concentration Camp Bergen Belsen) exists. Lists also include maiden name, date and place of birth and date of death, if known, but not religion. It also names many survivors who died some months after liberation.
Buchenwald	Buchenwald, in Thuringia, was one of the earlier concentration camps. The US National Archives has an extensive collection of records from this camp.
Dachau	Dachau was the earliest major concentration camp. Two books have been published listing some of those who died there. The National Archives in College Park, Maryland, USA and in New York have film containing personnel records from Dachau. Also: Dachau Foundation in Dachau has computerised all Dachau records and researchers may write to: Dachau KZ Gedenkstätte, Alte Romerstrasse 75, Dachau, Germany.
Flossenbürg Germany Bavaria	Flossenbürg did not contain many prisoners until 1943. Between 1943 and 1945, however, nearly 97,000 persons, including about 10,000 Jews - mostly from Hungary and Poland, were sent there and about 30,000 persons died in the camp or in the death marches, which took place near the end of the War.
Gross-Rosen Poland	In 1992 the Gross Rosen Museum issued Ksiega Zmarlych Wiezniow K1, Gross Rosen. This book lists 8,887 names. Write to: ul Starchowicka 9a, 58-300 Walbrzych, Poland.
Izbica	Thousands of German and Austrian Jews were sent to Izbica, which mainly acted as a collection camp. Most persons were then transferred to killing centres. There are no lists of people who died there or in the death camps of Chelmno, Sobibor or Treblinka.
Lodz	Records of the Lodz ghetto exist - 5 volumes were published under the title 'Lodz - Names'. Many may have lost their lives after the ghetto was liquidated in 1944 and inmates were sent to other camps.
Ravensbrück	Ravensbrück was primarily a concentration camp for women but it held about 20,000 men too. Prisoners came from all over Europe, with about 20% from Germany, although most of the German prisoners seem to have been non-Jews. The US Holocaust Memorial Museum has four reels of film listing transport to and from Ravensbrück. Researchers may also write to: Mahn und Gedenkstaette Ravensbrück, Strasse der Nationen 1, D 16798 Fuerstenberg/Havel, Germany. The records are in chronological order of transports with no index of names. It may therefore be difficult to find information.

Sachsenhausen	Like Buchenwald, this camp, which was situated just north of Berlin, was used after Kristallnacht to hold German Jews, most of whom were later released. The Russians seized virtually all the records, and copies are kept in the US Holocaust Memorial Museum.
Theresienstadt (Terezin)	Theresienstadt had excellent records on all persons sent there, and those transferred to other camps. Virtually complete records are held at: Terezin Museum, Pamatnik Terezin, 411 55 Terezin, Czech Republic. E-mail: archiv@pamatnik-terezin.cz. See Web site: http://www.jewishgen.org/bohmor/czechguide.html Also: Beth Theresienstadt, Givat Haim-Ihud, Mobile Poste Emek Hefer, 38935, Israel. E-mail: bterezin@inter.net.il Web site: http://www.cet.ac.il/terezin. Complete files are available on the fate of those interned there. They include, for the most part, name, maiden name, date of birth, place, if further transported to another camp, transport number and whether they survived.
Minsk and Maly Trostinec	These were not concentration camps in the usual sense of the word. The Minsk ghetto had two parts. One part held largely local Jewish residents. In addition, about 35,000 Jews from Austria, Bohemia, Germany and Moravia were sent either to Minsk or Maly Trostinec. Most persons were murdered within a few days of arrival. There are virtually no victim lists for either Maly Trostinec or Minsk, other than the records relating to their transportation there. Very few survived.

FURTHER INFORMATION
Stammbaum
This Journal of German-Jewish Genealogical Research contains a special feature entitled *'Mostly Holocaust: Sources & Resources'* compiled by Peter Landé, which appeared in volume 13 issued in May 1998. (See page 58 for further details.)

Internet
A very useful Internet site 'German/Austrian Holocaust-Related Databases on the Web' compiled by Peter Landé is at:
http://www.jewishgen.org/GerSig/holocaust.htm. It gives some short explanations about various databases and their Internet addresses where information on some of the memorial (yizkor) books can be searched on-line.

In addition, there is a book entitled *'How to Document Victims and Locate Survivors of the Holocaust'* by Gary Mokotoff, Avotaynu, 1995. The book describes the major sources of information such as the Pages of Testimony, International Tracing Service and yizkor books as well as sources unique to specific geographical localties. There is also a chapter on how to locate survivors. A major portion of the book is available on the Internet at http://www.avotaynu.com/Holocaust.

MUSEUMS
Imperial War Museum, Holocaust Exhibition
Lambeth Road, London, SE1 6HZ.
Tel: 020 7416 5320 - Fax: 020 7416 5374
E-mail: books@iwm.org.uk
Four years in the making, the Imperial War Museum's Holocaust Exhibition uses historical material to tell the story of the Nazis' persecution of the Jews and other groups before and during the Second World War. The 1200 square metre historical display covers two floors and brings to this country for the first time rare and important artefacts, some of them from former concentration and extermination camp museums in Germany, Poland and the Ukraine.

The Holocaust Centre, Beth Shalom
Laxton, Newark, Notts. NG22 OPA.
Tel: 01623 836627 - Fax: 01623 836647
E-mail: office@bethshalom.com   Web site: http://www.bethshalom.com
An important educational study centre, library and exhibition on the history of the Holocaust set up and built attached to their home by members of the Smith family. The Centre, which has also published a number of books of Holocaust survivor testimonies, is not open to the general public, but only to pre-booked groups. To visit you should arrange to join a group. For further information contact them at the above address. In addition the Centre has a mail-order book service for Holocaust publications and educational resources.

Note: The Imperial War Museum and Beth Shalom are not equipped to handle individual research inquiries.

ARCHIVES IN GERMANY
Most Town or State Archives have documents relating to the Holocaust. What is available varies from place to place. (Main details of archives are to be found under 'Useful Addresses' on page 27.)

Stiftung 'Neue Synagoge Berlin - Centrum Judaicum'
Oranienburgerstrasse 28/30, D-10117, Berlin.
Holds many records of the former 'Reichsvereinigung der deutschen Juden', which include deportation lists as well as 'Heimeinkäufe für Theresienstadt', ie legal documents detailing lists of assets and properties, which individuals had to 'sell' before their deportation. (Further details to be found on pages 17,28,36.)

Acknowledgement: We are exceedingly grateful to Peter Landé for allowing us the use, in this section, of his published data.

USEFUL ADDRESSES

ARCHIVES

The various 'Länder' (States) of Germany, each have their own 'Landesarchiv' or 'Staatsarchiv' (State Archive), all holding information on Jews and Jewish communities in their particular area. What is available depends on what has survived the Nazi period, as the Nazi authorities confiscated birth, marriage and death registers of Jewish communities and other records. In 1944/45, on the orders of the 'Reichssippenhauptamt', the registers continued to be photocopied.

Records can also be found in the appropriate archive of the town (Stadtarchiv), in some villages (Gemeindearchiv) or in private archives of former rulers of the numerous former independent territories which existed up to the 19th century. A book: 'Taschenbuch für Familiengeschichtsforschung' (Pocket book for genealogical research) alphabetically lists public and private archives in Germany.

Most archives and libraries in Germany have copies of the memorial books of victims of the Holocaust issued by the German Government in 1986.

When writing to an archive in Germany, one should enclose one or two International reply coupons (which are available from any Post Office) and if possible, write in German, or get someone to write the letter for you. German archives are, in general, well organised, and the staff are helpful and friendly. However, do not be discouraged if you occasionally receive no reply to a letter of enquiry.

Bundesarchiv (German Federal Archive)
The headquarters of the Bundesarchiv are in Koblenz, and there are branches in the following towns and cities: Aachen, Bayreuth, Berlin (see below), Bonn, Frankfurt/Main, Freiburg, Rastatt and St. Augustin. It is best to write to the branch nearest to the town where your ancestors came from.
Web site: http://www.bundesarchiv.de.

BERLIN
Bundesarchiv,
Finckensteinallee 63, 12205 Berlin
The German Federal Archive - the equivalent of the Public Record Office in Britain, has microfilms of German-Jewish records, mainly from the 19th century. It also has some other items, e.g. lists of Jews who acquired Prussian nationality in the early 19th century. There are some records from the former East Germany.

ARCHIVES IN GERMANY

All archives in Germany hold some material of interest to Jewish genealogists. Information available depends on what has survived after the Holocaust. The table below mentions only a few of the many archives in Germany. Unfortunately they are too numerous to list them all.

LÄNDER (STATES)	ADDRESS/INFORMATION
Baden-Württemberg	**STAATLICHE ARCHIVVERWALTUNG** (State Archive Stuttgart) Eugenstrasse 7, D-70182 Stuttgart. Tel: +49 711 212 4335 - Fax: +49 711 212 4360 E-mail: Landesarchivdirektion@lad-bw.de **BADEN-WÜRTTEMBERG STATE ARCHIVE STUTTGART** Konrad-Adenauerstrasse 4, D-70173 Stuttgart. Tel: +49 711 212 4320 - Fax: +49 711 2121 4360 E-mail: Hauptstaatarchiv@s.lad-bw.de Web site: http//www.lad-bw.de **GENERALLANDESARCHIV KARLSRUHE** Nordliche Hildapromenade 2, D-76133 Karlsruhe Tel: +49 721 926 2251 - Fax: +49 721 929 2231 E-mail: generallandesarchiv@glaka.lad-bw.de
Bayern (Bavaria)	See page 30 for details
Berlin	**LANDESARCHIV BERLIN,** Kalckreuthstrasse 1-2, 10777 Berlin. Tel: +49 30 2 1283 0 - Fax: +49 30 2 1283 177 E-mail: info@landesarchiv-berlin.de **Information:** The Berlin City Archives have records of Berlin Jews who were deported to concentration camps during the Holocaust, including documentation of seizure of assets and other material relating to the Jews and the Jewish community of Berlin. **STIFTUNG 'NEUE SYNAGOGE BERLIN** - Centrum Judaicum' - Archives, Oranienburgerstrasse 28/30, D-10117 Berlin **Archive:** The archive holds some material on the Jewish community of Berlin. Indexes contain lists of members of the Berlin Jewish community with voting rights for the years 1883, 1886, 1889, 1892, 1898, 1904, 1907, 1910 and 1913. These give names, addresses and occupations. 'Judenbürgerbücher der Stadt Berlin 1809-1851' (books of Jewish citizens of Berlin 1809-1851) with some appendices for other years. Jewish marriages in Berlin for the years 1723-1759 and for 1759-1813. Information on various people persecuted by the Nazis on racist grounds who, after 1945, were recognised as 'Opfer des Fascismus' (Victims of Fascism). Some of the documents of the former 'Gesamtarchiv der Juden in Deutschland' (Central Archives of Jews in Germany) in Berlin of German Jewish communities and organisations, which had been taken by the Nazis, have survived in Germany and have now been returned to the Centrum Judaicum Archives. These include some records of the former Prussian province Posen

Berlin continued	(Poznan/Posen). Because of the German 'Datenschutz' (Data Protection law) some of the material cannot be seen personally. Other parts of the former archive found in various parts of Germany or smuggled out just before the war by the family of the last archivist, are now at the Leo Baeck Institute in New York (see page 31) and in the Central Archives for the History of the Jewish People in Jerusalem (see page 32.)
Brandenburg	**LANDESHAUPTARCHIV BRANDENBURG** An der Orangerie 3, D-14469, Potsdam. Tel: +49 331 5674 120 - Fax: +49 331 5674 112 **Information:** Some information is available on Jews in the province of Brandenburg as well as some pre-1874 civil registration records for Berlin.
Bremen	**STAATSARCHIV BREMEN,**Am Staatsarchiv 1, D-28203, Bremen. Tel: +49 421 361 6221
Hamburg	**STAATSARCHIV HAMBURG** Kattunbleiche 19, D-22041 Hamburg. Tel: +49 40 3681 3200 - Fax: +49 40 3681 3201
Hessen (Hesse)	**HESSISCHES HAUPTSTAATSARCHIV,** Mosbacherstrasse 55, 65187 Wiesbaden. Tel: +49 611 881 0 - Fax: +49 611 881 145 E-mail: postelle@hhstaw.hessen.de **JÜDISCHES MUSEUM DER STADT FRANKFURT/MAIN (Archives)** Untermainkai 14-15, 60311 Frankfurt-am-Main **Information:** This museum has large archives and also houses the Brilling Collection, a private archive of a very large collection of German-Jewish material collected by the late Rabbi Bernhard Brilling and donated by his wife to the Frankfurt museum. Among the holdings is material on pre-war Jewish communities of former East Germany, Pomerania, Posen (Poznan) and Silesia, and on various other parts of West Germany and some family histories. The collection is uncatalogued and mostly still in storage. Written application is required to see it. The museum has copies of all Jewish microfilms held by the Bundesarchiv, and is smaller and more easily accessible.
Mecklenburg-Vorpommern (Mecklenburg Western Pomerania)	**LANDESHAUPTARCHIV SCHWERIN,** Graf-Schack-Allee 2, 19053 Schwerin. Tel: +49 385 5929 610-Fax: +49 385 5929 612 E-mail: LHA.schwerin@t-online.de **VORPOMMERSCHES LANDESARCHIV** Martin-Andersen-Nexö-Platz 1, 17489 Greifswald. Tel: +49-383 4772 86 E-mail: LAGreifswald@t-online.de
Niedersachsen (Lower Saxony)	**NIEDERSÄCHSES HAUPTSTAATSARCHIV,** Am Archiv 1, 30169, Hannover. Tel:+49 511 106 6601-Fax:+49 511 106 6699
Nordrhein-Westfalen (North Rhine Westphalia)	**NORDRHEIN-WESTFÄLISCHES HAUPTSTAATSARCHIV** Mauerstrasse 55, 40476 Düsseldorf. Tel: +49 211 944902 - Fax: +49 211 9447002
Rheinland-Pfalz (Rheinland-Palatinate)	**LANDESHAUPTARCHIV KOBLENZ,** Karmelitestrasse 1/3, 56068 Koblenz. Tel: +49 261 91290
Saarland	**LANDESARCHIV SAARBRÜCKEN,** Scheidter Strasse 114, 66123 Saarbrücken. Tel: +49 681 399953
Sachsen (Saxony)	**SÄCHSISCHES STAATSARCHIV LEIPZIG,** Schongauerstrasse 1, D-04329 Leipzig. Tel: +49 341 255 5500

Sachsen (Saxony) continued	**Information:** This archive has some civil records for the five 'new Länder' (formerly East Germany), as well as for some territories which had been part of Germany before World War II. **SÄCHSISCHES HAUPTSTAATSARCHIV DRESDEN** Archivstrasse 14, 01097 Dresden. Tel: +49 351 567 1274 - Fax: +49 351 802 1274 E-mail: hstadd@hsta.smi.sachen.de **STADTARCHIV DRESDEN** Marienallee 3, D-01099, Dresden **STATE ARCHIVE LEIPZIG** Beethovenstrasse 4, D-04107, Leipzig.
Saxony-Anhalt	**LANDESHAUPTARCHIV SACHSEN-ANHALT MAGDEBURG** Hegelstrasse 25, 39104 Magdeburg. Tel: +49 391 5664 3 - Fax: +49 391 5664 440
Schleswig-Holstein	**LANDESARCHIV SCHLESWIG-HOLSTEIN** Schloss Gottdorf (Prinzenpalais), 24837 Schleswig. Tel: +49 4621 86 1800 - Fax: +49 4621 86 1801 E-mail: LASH-SL@t-online.de
Thüringen (Thuringia)	**THÜRINGISCHES HAUPTSTAATSARCHIV WEIMAR** Marstallstrasse 2, 99423 Weimar. Tel: +49 3643 3933 - Fax: +49 3643 3936 E-mail: thhstaweimar@thueringen.de

ARCHIVES IN BAVARIA

In 1948/49 photocopies of the Jewish birth, marriage and death registers of Jewish communities in Bavaria were made, mainly for compensation purposes. There had been two complete volumes and one incomplete. In 1953, on the instructions of the Ministry of Finance, these photocopies were transferred from the Bavarian 'Landesentschädigungsamt' (Restitution Office). The complete volumes were transferred to the Bavarian State Archives. The incomplete volume had been handed over to the 'Landesverband der Jüdischen Kultusgemeinden' (Association of Jewish Communities). Many of these documents and records are now in Israel, in the Central Archives for the History of the Jewish People in Jerusalem.

Bavarian Central State Archives Munich
Schönfeldstrasse 5-11, D-08539 Munich
Tel: +49 89 28638-482 - Fax: +49 89 28638-615

Mittelfranken (Middle Franconia)
State Archive Nuremberg (Nürnberg) Archivstrasse 17, D-90408 Nuremberg
Archives for Mittelfranken (Middle Franconia). Historical material, records and historical documents of former Jewish communities in the area, also old Jewish birth, marriage and death registers for towns and villages in Mittelfranken.

Oberbayern (Upper Bavaria)
State Archive Munich, Postfach 22 11 52, D-80501, Munich

Oberfranken (Upper Franconia)
State Archive Bamberg, Hainstrasse 39, D-96947 Bamberg

Oberpfalz (Upper Palatine)
State Archive Regensburg, Keplestr.1, 93047 Regensburg

Schwaben (Swabia)
State Archive Augsburg, Salomon-Idler-Strasse 2, Augsburg

Unterfranken (Lower Franconia)
State Archive Würzburg, Residenzplatz, 2, D-97070, Würzburg
Archives for Unterfranken (Lower Franconia) hold historical records and documents
of former Jewish communities in the area. In addition, they hold copies of Jewish
birth, marriage and death registers as well as some Gestapo documents for
Würzburg.

Jüdisches Dokumentationszentrum, Würzburg
Valentin-Beckerstr. 11, Würzburg
Tel: +49 931 18275
This is part of the Stadt Archiv Würzburg. It is situated in premises of the Jewish
Old Age Home. Most of the material of Jewish interest held in the Stadt Archiv is
gradually being transferred here. It covers the whole of the district 'Unterfranken'
(Lower Franconia).

Town and Village Archives
For people researching other parts of Germany, it should be possible to address
letters to:
STADTARCHIV and the name of the town or GEMEINDEARCHIV for smaller
places. Enclose an international reply coupon.

University Archives
Universities have archives going back many years. If a person attended or obtained
a degree from a certain university it is worthwhile writing to them for information.

Private Archives
There are a number of private archives, maintained by the families of the former
rulers of the numerous independent territories which existed in Germany in the 18th
and the beginning of the 19th century, which hold valuable information for the
Jewish genealogist.

ARCHIVES IN OTHER PARTS OF THE WORLD
U.S.A.
Leo Baeck Institute
15 West 16th Street, New York, 10011.
Tel: +1 212 744 6400 - Fax: +1 212 988 1305
E-mail: lbi1@lbi.com   Web site: http://www.lbi.com (cont.)
The Leo Baeck Institute in New York, with branches in London and Jerusalem, was
founded in 1955 and named after a leading Berlin rabbi. It is one of the most
valuable places for German Jewish genealogy. It has a lot of information,

documents etc. of German Jewish interest. Much of the former 'Gesamtarchiv der Juden in Deutschland' (Central Archive of Jews in Germany) is deposited here. The Institute also houses the Berthold Rosenthal as well as the Rudolf Simonis Archives.These are two former professional genealogists who produced family trees for many families, some going back several centuries. The Institute collects family histories and material. It also publishes 'Stammbaum' - the Journal of German-Jewish Genealogical Research' (for further details see page 58).

ISRAEL
Central Archives for the History of the Jewish People (see page 18)
Sprinzak Building, Hebrew University, Givat Ram, Jerusalem, Israel.
Tel: +972 2 635 716
The archives are situated in the basement of the Sprinzak Building of the Hebrew University. It is the largest Jewish archive in the world, and was founded by Immigrants from Germany. There is a lot of material here, once one is able to find one's way through the various indexes. As far as former German communities are concerned, there are many original documents, e.g. records of organisations and synagogues, newspapers and magazines relating to certain personalities or families, some family histories. Many documents are on microfilm. There are also some miniature photocopies of birth, marriage and death registers bound together in tiny paperback books. Although magnifiers are available, it is advisable to take a good magnifier to decipher these.

The archive also has some of the surviving material of the former 'Gesamtarchiv der Juden in Deutschland' (Central Archives of Jews in Germany), other parts of this being in the Leo Baeck Institute, New York (see page 31) and the Stiftung Neue Synagogue - Centrum Judaicum in Berlin (see page 28). It also houses various materials on many Jewish communities in the former Prussian province of Posen (Poznan).

LIBRARIES
GERMANY
Bibliothek des Jüdischen Gemeindehauses (Jewish Community Centre)
Fasenenstrasse 79/80, 10623 Berlin
Built on the site of a synagogue which received a visit from Kaiser Wilhelm II soon after it opened in 1912, was damaged on Kristallnacht and later bombed during World War II. The Jewish community centre has a very good library on all subjects of Jewish interest, books on former Jewish communities, Jewish magazines worldwide as well as Israeli newspapers. The Centre also has a kosher restaurant and exhibitions are held in the foyer.

Bibliothek Jüdisches Museum Franken (Library)
Nürnbergerstrasse 3, D-90762 Fürth
Specialises in books relating to the history of Jewish communities in Southern Germany.

Deutsche Staatsbibliothek
Potsdamer Strasse 33, 10785 Berlin and Unter den Linden 8, 10117 Berlin
The German state library has some Jewish books (in German) and directories.

Humboldt University Library
Dorotheenstrasse 27, 10117, Berlin
This library has a large collection of Jewish books (mostly in German).
Web site: http://www.ub.hu-berlin.de

Institut für die Geschichte der deutschen Juden
Rothenbaumchaussee 7, 20148 Hamburg
Excellent library.

LONDON
The German Historical Institute - Library
17 Bloomsbury Square, London, WC1A 2LP.
Tel: 020 7404 5486 - Fax: 020 7404 5573
E-mail: library-ghil@ghil.co.uk
Web site: http://www.ghil.co.uk
The library has about 58,000 volumes and focuses on German history from the reformation time onwards, with emphasis on the Nazi period and post-war Germany. The library has an outstanding collection of books about the Holocaust, mainly secondary literature, but also source material. The library is a reference library only but with photocopy facilities. Open Monday-Friday.

Goethe Institute Library & Information Centre
50 Prince's Gate, Exhibition Road, London, SW7 2PH.
Tel: 020 7596 4040 (Issue desk) - 020 7596 4044 (Information service)
E-mail: library@london.goethe.org
Web site: http://www.goethe.de/london
This is not an archive library and therefore has very little which would assist in genealogical research. However, they do have a small section of books on German-Jewish history and, in addition, try to present an up-to-date picture of modern Germany, which may be of help to some people who are researching in this field.

The Jewish Genealogical Society of Great Britain (Library)
Finchley Synagogue, Kinloss Gardens, London, N3 2SY.
(Access for Members only.) The Society has a German Special Interest Group. For details of the library, please access our Web site: http://www.jgsgb.ort.org. The Library holds a very large collection of yizkor (memorial) books and donations are greatly appreciated. (For details of the Society see page 37).

Leo Baeck Institute, London
4 Devonshire Street, London, W1N 2BH
Tel: 020 7580 3493 - Fax: 020 7436 8634
E-mail: ap@lbilon.demon.co.uk
Leo Baeck Institute year books are available in the London Wiener Library (see page 22 for details) on the first floor of the building.

London School of Jewish Studies (formerly Jews' College)
Jews' College Library, Schaller House, 44a Albert Road, London, NW4 2SJ.
Tel: 020 8203 6427 - Fax: 020 8203 6420
E-mail: enquiries@lsjs.ac.uk

The library has some books on German Jews. (Browsing at the LSJS Library is now free to everyone - JGSGB members will no longer need a letter of introduction.)

ISRAEL
Jewish National and University Library
PO Box 503, Jerusalem 91004, Israel
Department of Manuscripts: Tel: +972 2 585 0555
Microfilm Room: Tel: +972 2 585 0222
Books in all languages, many on former Jewish communities.

Leo Baeck Institute
33 Bustanai Street, 91082 Jerusalem, Israel
Tel/Fax: +972 2 63 3790
E-mail: leobaeck@netvision.net.il   Web site: http://www.leobaeck.org

Wiener Library
Tel Aviv University, Ramat Aviv, Israel
Many older books, which were originally part of the Wiener Library in London, are now in the Wiener Library, which is located at the University in Tel Aviv. Holds the major part of the yizkor (memorial) book collection from the London Wiener Library.

U.S.A.
New York Public Library - Jewish Reference Division
5th Avenue and 42nd Street, New York City, 10018.
Web site: http://www.nypl.org/research/chss/jws/jewish.html
This unique institution contains a vast amount of material of interest to Jewish genealogists.

MUSEUMS
Historisches Museum Bremerhaven/Morgenstern Museum
An der Geeste, 27570 Bremerhaven
Tel: +49 471 2 01 38   Fax: +49 471 5 90 27 00
Web site: http://www.deutsche-auswanderer-datenbank.de/enframeset.htm
Deutsche Auswanderer-Datenbank (German Immigration Database) provides a searchable database of all European emigrants who immigrated to North America from German ports between 1820 and 1939. Sources are passenger lists. The current database may be searched at the Museum in Bremerhaven or by mail for a fee.

Jüdisches Museum Berlin
Lindenstrasse 9-14, D-10969 Berlin
This controversial new museum, which was designed by the architect Daniel Libeskind is due to be opened in 2001, will feature an interactive learning centre, archives and a research department.

Jüdisches Museum Franken in Fürth
Königstrasse 89, D-90762 Fürth
Museum opened in 1999 in an old Jewish house, with its own mikva and succah. The Jewish history of the house goes back to 1622.

Jüdisches Museum Franken in Schnaittach
Museumsgasse 12-16, D-91220 Schnaitach
Schnaittach is in Bavaria, north-east of Nuremberg, on the road from Lauf to Bayreuth. The museum is housed in the beautiful old building of the Synagogue (going back to 1570) and the adjoining house of the Rabbi and Cantor.

Museum Judengasse Am Börneplatz Frankfurt/Main
Intersection of Battonnstrasse and Karl-Schumacher-Strasse, Frankfurt/Main
Tel: +49 69 297 7419
The Museum has a computerised InfoBank, which is used to trace Frankfurt Jews who died in the Holocaust. (See under Cemeteries, as the oldest Jewish cemetery in Frankfurt adjoins this museum.)

Jüdisches Museum der Stadt Frankfurt/Main
Untermainkai 14-15, 60311 Frankfurt/Main
Museum established in the former residence of the Rothschild banking family of Frankfurt. The museum also has large archives. (For details see Archives page 29.)

Museum für Hamburgische Geschichte (Hamburg History Museum)
Holstenwall, 24, Hamburg.
Tel: +49 40 3504 2360/80
The museum has passenger lists for all ships which sailed from Hamburg from the mid-19th century until 1917.

SYNAGOGUES

BELSIZE SQUARE SYNAGOGUE
Henry Kuttner, Librarian/Archivist, **(By appointment only)**
Belsize Square Synagogue, 51 Belsize Square, London NW3 4HX
Tel: 020 7794 3949 - Fax: 020 7431 4559
E-mail: belsqsyn@aol.com   Web site: http://www.synagogue.org.uk
Belsize Square Synagogue (Independent) is the home of the community formed in 1939 by refugees from continental Europe, mostly German-speaking. The Synagogue library holds some 1500 books of Jewish interest, split into about 30 categories, including a section devoted to the Jews of Germany and Austria.

For genealogical interest, the library holds two enormous volumes of the 'Gedenkbuch der Deutschen Juden', which was published by the German government in 1986 of German Jews who perished. These books give names in alphabetical order, plus first names, dates and place of birth, dates and place of death (if known). In addition there is a similar book giving details of the Austrian Jews who were deported to Terezin (Theresienstadt); and a book giving details of the children of French origin who perished.

Unfortunately, the Synagogue database does not have details of its members' family history. However any bona fide requests received will be dealt with as well as they can. Should anyone be interested in a particular Jewish surname, or anything relating to the above, they may contact Mr. Henry Kuttner (address above) who will see whether he has a member with that name, and ask that member if he/she wishes to be contacted by you.

Stiftung 'Neue Synagoge Berlin - Centrum Judaicum' - (see pages 28/29 for Archives) Oranienburgerstrasse 28/30, D-10117 Berlin.
Tel: +49 30 880 28451 - Fax: +49 30 282 1176
E-mail: cjudaicum@snafu.de   Web site: http://www.cjudaicum.de/
The synagogue with its Byzantine architecture and beautiful gilded dome miraculously escaped destruction on the night of 9/10 November 1938, 'Kristallnacht', owing to the immediate intervention of the Police Superintendent of the district. [1]As the synagogue had been classed as a Protected Historical Monument since the reign of Emperor William I, he immediately marched to the Synagogue with a troop of police and the fire service of the district, carrying the Official Order of Protection of the Monument in his hand. Referring to the document he prevented the SA (Brown Shirts) from lighting further fires and, at the same time, summoned fire engines, immediately extinguishing the fire already lit.' ([1]Hermann Simon in his preface to the 1987 reissue of Ludwig Geiger's 'Geschichte der Juden in Berlin'.) Very little damage had been done. During an air attack in February 1943 the synagogue was however hit and badly damaged. The main part was demolished in the 1950's, leaving only the front standing. This part of the building and the dome has been restored, and the dome is once again a distinctive Berlin landmark. Next door is a modern building containing offices, library and archives, and there is a small museum in the remains of the old building.

© Thea Skyte

GENEALOGICAL SOCIETIES

GERMANY
Deutsche Zentralstelle für Genealogie, Schongauer Strasse 1, D-04329 Leipzig
This is the German equivalent of the Society of Genealogists in Great Britain. It has some German-Jewish records on microfilm. Bear in mind that the Jews were never more than 1% of the total German population. In 1933, there were 600,000 Jews out of 60 million Germans. Today there are 50,000 Jews (in 77 Jewish communities) out of 80 million.

It has some civil records for the five 'new Länder' (formerly East Germany), as well as for some territories which had been part of Germany before World War II and are now in Poland or Russia.
Web site: http://www.genealogy.net/gene/www/ghlp/dzfg-de.html

Hamburger Gesellschaft für jüdische Genealogie
c/o Jürgen Sielemann, Staatsarchiv Hamburg, Kattunbleiche 19, D-22041 Hamburg
The Society does not undertake research of non-Hamburg families.

ISRAEL
Dorot, Beth Hatefutsoth, Tel Aviv.
A Jewish Genealogical Centre is established here. The Centre requests that family trees should be deposited with them, which will then be put onto a computer. These trees are being amalgamated with those submitted to the International Association of Jewish Genealogical Societies (IAJGS) and those on the Web pages on JewishGen. They can be accessed on the Internet on JewishGen's 'Family Tree of the Jewish People'.

U.K.
Anglo-German Family History Society
14 River Reach, Teddington, Middlesex. TW11 9QL.
Tel/Fax: 020 8977 2731
On joining the Society, new members are sent a booklet explaining the various services which members of the Society are entitled to use. Among these are Len Metzner Indexes, German telephone directories and the Württemberg Indexes.

The Jewish Genealogical Society of Great Britain
PO Box 13288, London, N3 3WD.
E-mail: jgsgb@ort.org   Web site: http://www.jgsgb.ort.org
(Membership Secretary: JGSGB, PO Box 27061, London, N2 0GT)
The Society has introduced Special Interest Groups (SIGs). These meet at various times during the year (details are given in the Society's Newsletter). The aim of the groups is to bring members together in order to help one another with their research and to learn from each other's experiences. The Society has the following SIGs: Anglo-Jewish, Dutch, German, Latvian, Lithuanian and joint Poland & Galicia. In addition, membership of the Society includes: monthly meetings, family history workshops, library (see page 33), mentoring, journal and newsletter. (A membership application form is in the centre of the guide).

OTHER

GERMAN NATIONAL TOURIST OFFICE
P.O. Box 2695, London W1A 3TN.
Tel: 020 7317 0908 - Fax: 020 7495 6129
Web site: http://www.germany-tourism.de
E-mail: German_National_Tourist_Office@compuserve.com
'Germany for the Jewish Traveller', obtainable free of charge from:

The Consulate of the Federal Republic of Germany,
871 UN Plaza, New York, NY 10017
E-mail: German-Mission-Consulate-GIC-1@netlink1.net.

It gives a short history of Jews in Germany and information and addresses of museums, synagogues and sites of Jewish interest in a number of German towns. In addition, 'From Horror to Hope - Germany, the Jews and Israel' is an interesting book on the history of the Jews in Germany from medieval to the present.

The Jewish Genealogical Society of Great Britain
Registered Charity No 1022738

- Valuable expert guidance in research

- Regular gatherings to meet others interested in genealogy

- Access to our growing library

- *SHEMOT and NEWSLETTER,* our quarterly publications, full of helpful advice and information

- Information on other societies all over the world and access to thousands of people interested in Jewish genealogy

- Use of the International Jewish Family Finder available at meetings

- Information on our web-site and our e-mail messaging system

- Access to our own Family Finder giving names being researched by our members

Join us for an exciting journey discovering your personal family history. Begin by interviewing relatives, studying old photographs and family documents and then ..... what next?

Our society was formed in 1992 with beginners and experienced researchers joining forces.

- to help one another to learn and discover more about genealogy

- to encourage genealogical research

- to promote the preservation of Jewish genealogical records and resources

- to share information amongst members

The society is open to all interested in Jewish genealogy and is constituted on a wholly secular basis.

We have an extensive programme of events, including regular monthly members' meetings, lectures with specialist speakers, and visits to places of genealogical interest. Special Interest Groups research particular countries and the art of writing a Family History. Our annual all-day seminar attracts excellent speakers, well known as experts in their fields. Regional groups of members arrange meetings in their own areas.

We lead the Family History Workshops held by the Jewish Museum at the Steinberg Centre in Finchley, and at other venues. We also provide speakers for educational meetings at schools and synagogues and panels for social events, often in conjunction with other charities.

Our journal, SHEMOT (Names), was the 1998 winner of the International Association of Jewish Genealogical Societies' Outstanding Publication award. Published quarterly, it contains a variety of articles of interest to genealogists, book reviews, abstracts of overseas genealogical journals, practical research tips, and useful addresses. We are keen to publish members' own articles.

We have a lively Newsletter, also published quarterly, giving news about the Society and forthcoming events, international genealogical affairs, computer activities, including our web Site, library notes, members' letters and queries and lists of new members.

Our reference library of books, research papers, microfiches and journals from other societies around the world is being built up. It includes one of the largest collection of Yizkor (memorial) books in the U.K., covering many of the destroyed communities in Europe, and many family trees, indexed by principal surnames, compiled by our members. The library is open to members before meetings and at other regular times announced in advance.

We now have two guides under the general heading of Jewish Ancestors ? - A Beginner's Guide to Jewish Genealogy in Great Britain, and A Guide to Jewish Genealogy in Germany & Austria. A third, A Guide to Jewish Genealogy in Latvia & Estonia, is expected to be ready in March 2001. The Beginner's guide is packed from cover to cover with useful information, indispensable for everyone, beginner or expert, whilst the others give valuable information on the archives in each area and how to obtain the records you thought no longer existed. The guide on Latvia & Estonia also gives useful tips for the genealogical traveller.

Our web site, www.jgsgb.ort.org, has pages covering the programme, membership, SHEMOT, (including a list of published articles), the library (including the catalogue), useful links, and a repository of files contributed by members and available for down-loading.

We have two e-mail addresses: jgsgb@ort.org for general enquiries and jgsgbmem@ort.org for membership related enquiries. An electronic mailing list has also been set up, so that messages can easily (and extremely cheaply) be sent to every member on the list, whilst preserving their anonymity.

The society is run by volunteers who give time, effort and expertise. We can always use more help.

We cannot undertake paid research, but we can give general advice and sometimes help with specific points of difficulty. Genealogical enquiries may be sent to:

The Genealogical Enquiries Officer
The Jewish Genealogical Society of Great Britain
PO Box 13288
LONDON N3 3WD

The Jewish Genealogical Society of Great Britain
Registered Charity No 1022738

Application for membership
and Gift Aid Declaration

Forenames ....

Surname ....

Address ....

....

.... Postcode ....

Tel... Fax ....

E-mail ....

To join please send a remittance made payable to The Jewish Genealogical Society of Great Britain to the Membership Secretary, The Jewish Genealogical Society of Great Britain, PO Box 27061 London N2 OGT.

Membership (see over) £ ....

Additional donation £ ....

Back numbers of SHEMOT (see over)
  Packs: A B C D (please circle which)
  Single copies (please state which) £ ....

Guides (see over)
  Beginner's, Germany & Austria, Latvia & Estonia £ ....
  (please circle which)

TOTAL £ ....

Reclaiming tax
(All who pay U.K. income tax or capital gains tax, including overseas residents, should tick this box. It costs you nothing and commits you to nothing. Remember to notify us if you no longer pay an amount of U.K. income tax or capital gains tax equal to the tax we reclaim on your donations, currently 28p for every £ you give)

Please reclaim tax under Gift Aid on all my donations to the Society made on or after 6th April 2000. ☐

Signature .... Date ....

or: I do not pay U.K. income tax or capital gains tax ☐

-3-

Subscriptions

(Please circle category)

	January to December	July to December	October to December next year
U.K. individual or institutional	£ 25.64	£ 12.82	£ 32.05
U.K. family	£ 32.05	£ 16.02	£ 40.06
U.K. reduced	£ 10.00	£ 5.00	£ 12.50
Overseas - individual or institutional - sterling	£ 25.00	£ 12.50	£ 31.25
Overseas - individual or institutional other	US$ 54.00	US$ 33.00	US$ 65.00

Those who sign a Gift Aid declaration may deduct tax, and so pay:

U.K. individual or institutional	£ 20.00	£ 10.00	£ 25.00
U.K. family	£ 25.00	£ 5.00	£ 31.25

U.K. residents who do not pay income tax or capital gains tax and charities may also pay at the lower rates.

Family subscriptions are for two people, one copy of SHEMOT etc. Reduced rate is for full time students, registered unemployed and others in similar circumstances. Overseas - sterling is for U.K. cheques and sterling drafts. Overseas - other is for other cheques and drafts. Institutional members do not receive membership lists or other information of a personal nature.

Shemot

Back numbers of SHEMOT are available as packs. Pack A covers 1992 to 1994, B 1995 to 1996, C 1997 to 1998 and D 1999 to 2000. Each pack contains eight issues, and costs £ 24.00 for each pack for despatch to U.K. addresses, £ 27.00 (UK cheques or sterling drafts) or US$ 44.00 (other cheques or drafts) for overseas. Single copies cost £ 4.00 each for U.K. addresses, £ 5.00 or US$ 8.00 for overseas.

Guides

The Society has now published two guides under the general heading Jewish Ancestors? . A Beginner's Guide to Jewish Genealogy in Great Britain, and a Guide to Jewish Genealogy in Germany & Austria. A third, A Guide to Jewish Genealogy in Latvia & Estonia, is expected to be ready in March 2001. Each guide costs £ 4.50U.K., £ 6.00 or US$ 10.00 overseas.

Confidentiality

We circulate a membership list to members only to help those with similar interests to contact each other more easily. Those who do not wish the list to include their full particulars should indicate below by circling the items they wish us to omit. Where details are withheld, a forwarding service, using the Society's Post Office box number, is available.

I wish my name/address/telephone/fax/e-mail address to be withheld

How did you hear of the Society?

....

Please return this form, with your remittance, to:

The Membership Secretary
The Jewish Genealogical Society of Great Britain
P0 Box 27061, London, N2 0GT

December 2000

CEMETERIES

BERLIN

Adass-Jisroel Cemetery
Wittlicher Strasse, Berlin-Weissensee
The cemetery of the orthodox Adass-Jisroel community in Berlin has been used since 1880. This cemetery was restored in 1985. In recent years students of the Humboldt-University in Berlin have prepared records to be housed in the restored gatehouse.

Cemetery of the Jewish Community of Berlin
Heerstrasse, Berlin-Grunewald
This cemetery was consecrated in 1955 and is now mainly used by the Jewish community of Berlin. It is part of a much larger non-Jewish cemetery.

Old Jewish Cemetery, Berlin
Schönhauser Allee 23-25, Berlin
This cemetery was used between 1827-1880, though some burials in family plots took place after this date. Records for most of the graves are at the office of the Weissensee cemetery - see below.

Jewish Cemetery, Frankfurt/Main
The cemetery is next to the Museum Judengasse am Börneplatz and is Frankfurt's oldest cemetery. Most of the graves were destroyed, however, there is a massive restoration project being undertaken to match the thousands of broken pieces of stone using a computer. To-date, 11,000 plaques have been inserted into the surrounding wall. Each plaque, lists the name, date of birth and place of death of the 11,000 Frankfurt Jews murdered in the Holocaust. (See section under Museums for further information)

Fürth Jewish Cemetery
Schlehenstrasse, Fürth
This cemetery opened in 1607 and is one of the largest and best preserved cemeteries in Germany.

Kippenheim-Schmieheim Cemetery
Located midway between the Black Forest and the River Rhine, the villages of Kippenheim and Schmieheim were home to Jews from the mid-17th century until 1939. The Schmieheim Cemetery, dating from the 17th century, is one of Germany's oldest. It was protected by townsfolk from Nazi gangs on Kristallnacht. Visitors should contact the Kippenheim Municipality.
Tel: +49-7825-9030 or +49-7825-1483

Lübeck Cemetery
The 300 year old cemetery is just outside the city. Visitors should contact Mr. Katz at the Lübeck Synagogue, St. Annenstrasse 11, Lübeck. Tel: +49 451 798 2182. If

the Synagogue is locked, Mr. Katz lives in an apartment building whose entrance is in the Synagogue grounds.

Magdeburg Jewish Cemetery
Fermesleber Weg 40-46, Magdeburg
The cemetery dates from the early 1800's.

Regensburg Cemetery
Schillerstrasse, Regensburg
This cemetery dates from 1822

Stuttgart Cemeteries
There are four Jewish cemeteries. For cemetery information please contact the Jewish Community of Baden-Württemberg. Tel: +49-711 228360.

Weissensee Cemetery
Herbert-Baum Strasse 45, D-13088 Berlin Weissensee. Tel: +49 30 9 65 33 30
The administration office at this address has complete records of all graves in this cemetery, which opened in 1880. It is the largest Jewish cemetery in western and central Europe (100 acres) and contains about 115,000 graves. It survived the Nazi era and the Second World War virtually undamaged. For some burials particulars of next of kin etc are also held. (See next page for map of cemetery).

Jewish Cemetery Worms
There are in the region of 2,000 graves in this cemetery. The lettering of many have survived since the first was erected in 1076. Many eminent scholars are buried here. The town's archivist, Dr. Illert, saved the cemetery and many Worms artefacts from the Nazis.

Jewish Cemeteries in other parts of Germany
These are too numerous to mention. They are under 'Denkmalschutz' (conservation order). Throughout Germany local individuals and organisations ensure that the cemeteries are very well looked after. A list of some of the cemetery projects is published in STAMMBAUM Issues 6-7 (December 1995), 8-9 (July 1996) and 14 (December 1998). In Baden-Württemberg the Landesdenkmalamt (Office for the preservation of historic memorials) has for some years been indexing Jewish cemeteries. Lists of German Jewish cemeteries can also be accessed through http://www.jewishgen.org/gersig and then go to 'Resources' and then 'Cemeteries'. The International Association of Jewish Genealogical Societies (IAJGS), is conducting a Jewish Cemetery Project; lists are on:
http://www.jewishgen.org/cemetery.

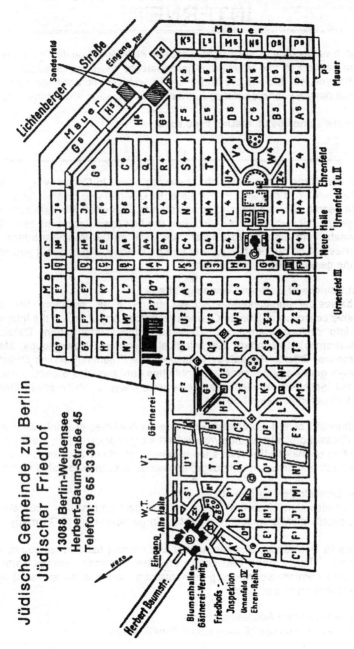

© Weissensee Cemetery, Berlin

INTERNET

The Internet has become a very useful source of information for genealogists; however don't expect to find your great-grandparents' marriage certificate on the Internet! What you will find are the addresses of archives, libraries etc. worldwide where you can pursue your researches further and information about their contents.

Listed below are some useful Internet Web sites:

Please note that some of the sites listed here are based in Germany and may be written in German. You can always translate the German into English by going to the AltaVista search engine's translation site at: http://babelfish.altavista.com. Here you may type the full web address (URL) into the box (don't forget the http://) and select 'Translate from German to English' and click on the translate button. The translation may not be perfect because of idiomatic and slang text, but you will be able to get the general idea of the content.

-◆-

The Internet Sources of German Genealogy site at: http://www.bawue.de/~hanacek/info/edatbase.htm - it is probably the most comprehensive collection of links to German resources anywhere on the Internet. It is divided into multiple categories: General/Regional Information; Databases (primarily surnames); Secondary Genealogical Resources; Newsgroups; Mailing Lists; Commercial Offers; Genealogy Software. The Frequently Asked Questions site: http://www.genealogy.net/gene/www/ghlp/tips.html provides a good primer for beginners, but there are excellent resources here, many of which are in German and can be translated as described above.

-◆-

The Federation of Eastern European Genealogical Societies presents its German Genealogy Cross-Index site at: http://www.feefhs.org/indexger.html. Here you will find a collection of links to the Web sites of a number of societies concerned with German research and/or German lineage, as well as links to maps of Germany.

-◆-

The German Genealogical Bridge at: http://www.geocites.com/SiliconValley/Haven/1538/german.html - contains a collection of excellent links, including a link to a large basic map of Germany.

It is important to learn about German names and naming patterns as you conduct your research. This may be seen on the German names site at: http://www.serve.com/shea/germusa/germname.htm, which is an excellent online reference resource on this subject.

-◆-

Germany: Telephone and Address Listings: http://www.ancestry.com/search/rectype/inddbs/4064.htm

No list of German Internet resources would be complete without the inclusion of the Germany GenWeb Project site at: http://www.rootsweb.com/~wggerman. The German site has been created and developed by volunteers wishing to expand the availability of free information on the Internet. There is a wealth of resources here too, ranging from general information, information about regions of Germany, historical maps, some passenger lists and information about the Kingdom of Prussia.

-◆-

I would like to thank George G. Morgan who wrote the above material which was published in the 'Ancestry Daily News', an electronic newsletter published by MyFamily.com and accessible at the Ancestry.com web site at: http://www.ancestry.com. I confirm that the above material is used by permission of the author and MyFamily.com. (Ed.RW)

Adalbert Goertz's Regional German FAQs
http://www3.adnc.com/~lynnd/gfaq.html
Very highly recommended

Addresses of Archives in Rhineland-Palatinate
http://www.koblenz.de/bildung/stadtarchiv/rpf-arch.html

Advice on Undertaking German Research at Libraries
and Archives in Baden-Württemberg
http://www.kinquest.com/genealogy/resources/badwue.html

Archives in Germany
http://my.bawue.de/~hanacek/info/earchive.htm
www.archiveschule.de (also with excellent links to many archives throughout the world)

Baden-Württemberg Map and Place Name Index
http://uk.multimap.com/index/GM3.htm

Baden-Württemberg State Archives
http://www.lad-bw.de

Bibliography of Books and Articles about Jewish History and Genealogy
http://ourworld.compuserve.com/homepages/German_Genealogy/hessbibl.htm

Black Forest Genealogy Web site
http://www.websters.net/blackforest

Cemeteries in Europe
http://www.totentanz.de/europe.htm

Das NS-Dokumentationszentrum (EL-DE-Haus)
http://www.museenkoeln.de/museenkoeln.de/ns-dok/fs_start.html
With interactive databank for the Jews of Koln Gedenkbuch (memorial book)

Federation of Eastern European Family History Societies
http://feefhs.org
This site contains details from all the societies. In addition to the Federation's pages, the site has a variety of historical maps of Eastern and Central Europe.

Genealogy at Beth Hatefutsoth in Israel
http://www.bh.org.il

German Genealogy: Home page
http://www.genealogy.net/gene
This provides some historical and geographical information on most of the German-speaking parts of Europe. The section entitled 'Regional Research' is indexed by the names of the states or former states.

German Genealogy: List of Documents and FAQs
http://www.genealogy.net/gene/faqs

German Genealogy: Tips for Researchers
http://www.genealogy.net/gene/misc/tips.html

German Migration Resource Centre
http://www.germanmigration.com
Encourages a worldwide exchange of genealogical information in connection with German emigrants and immigrants

Hamburg Passenger Lists
http://www.hamburg.de/LinkToYourRoots/english/lists.htm
This Web site includes the growing database of the Hamburg passenger lists of emigrant ships 1850-1934.

International Jewish Genealogical Society of France
http://www.chez.com/genami
Useful for Alsace research

Internet Sources of German Genealogy
http://main.amu.edu.pl/~rafalp/GEN/edatbase.htm

Jewish Communities of Germany
http://www.amyisrael.co.il/europe/germany/index.htm

JewishGen
http://www.jewishgen.org
Jewish Family Finder
Family Tree of the Jewish People (FTJP)

Databases:
Special Interest Groups on Bohemia and Moravia
http://www.jewishgen.org/BohMor
Includes information on some parts of Austria, particularly Vienna.
Special Interest Groups (SIGs), German (Gersig) home page
http://www.jewishgen.org/GerSIG/index.htm

LEO English-German Dictionary Online
http://dict.leo.org

Maps Gateway for Germany
http://www.entry.de

Memorials and Plaques of Bavarian Jewish Soldiers
http://www.historiker.de/projekte/hdbg/kriegsgraeber/english

Translations Page
http://babelfish.altavista.com

Zentralarchiv zur Erforschung der Geschichte der Juden in Deutschland (Central Archives for Research on the History of the Jews of Germany)
Bienenstrasse 5, 69117 Heidelberg, Germany
http://www.uni-heidelberg.de/institute
Post-war information on Jewish Communities and organisations. In addition, some deposits of family papers of a few well-known families.

Note: The Internet provides access to a wealth of information. Much of this information is not readily available in Great Britain and, before the advent of the Internet, would have been impractical to access. In addition the Internet offers the opportunity to correspond electronically by e-mail with others throughout the world at a fraction of the cost and with an immediacy not available by conventional mail. Having said this, although the computer is an excellent tool, it is important not to let it become your only interface with the world of genealogy. You will miss out on much of the enjoyment of tracing your family history if you do not also visit archives, examine original documents, and talk to relatives.

PART II
AUSTRIA

BORDERS

As you will see from the map below, Austria's borders changed considerably after the First World War. As a result, the Austro-Hungarian Empire was dramatically reduced in size.

Austria now consisted of Carinthia, Carniola, Lower Austria, Salzburg, Styria, Tyrol, Upper Austria and Vorarlberg and not all of these in their entirety. In 1921 it received from Hungary the area of Burgenland - being mostly German speaking - with the exception of the municipality of Sopron/Ödenburg and the immediate surrounding area. Hungary became an entirely separate country.

Czechoslovakia was newly formed from the Bohemian Crownlands and included Bohemia, Moravia and Austrian-Silesia plus Slovakia and Karpato-Ukraine, which was part of Upper-Hungary. In addition to this, existing neighbouring countries of Europe annexed several areas.

BORDERS

Before World War I _____
(Austria-Hungary)

Between the Wars
to end 1992. From
1 January 1993
Czechoslovakia   _ _ _ _ _
separated into
Slovakia and the
Czech Republic

46

STARTING YOUR RESEARCH

The first task of anyone researching their 'Austrian' ancestors is to determine from where in the vast Austro-Hungarian Empire the ancestors originated. For example, a census entry from 1880 may indicate the nationality as Austrian, but this could mean any number of cities that are now located in Austria, Bosnia, Croatia, the Czech Republic, Hungary, Italy, Poland, Romania, Slovakia, Slovenia or the Ukraine. **This section of the Guide concerns only research in what is now Austria,** meaning primarily the city of Vienna, which until 1938 was home to about 180,000 Jews, most of whom came from families who had emigrated from other parts of the Empire in the previous 150 years. If successful, your research of Austrian records should lead you to an ancestral town in one of the other parts of the Austro-Hungarian Empire.

VITAL RECORDS (Birth, Death and Marriage Records)
Israelitische Kultusgemeinde Wien (Jewish Community of Vienna)
Record books ('Matrikeln') of Jewish births, marriages and deaths in Vienna from the early 1800s to 1938 have survived and are owned by the Jewish Community of Vienna. These record books are to be found at the headquarters of the Vienna Jewish Community, which is located next to the only surviving synagogue in the centre of Vienna's first district. Inquiries are handled by the Department of Records, which is closed during holidays and at times during the summer. Inquiries by mail are acceptable, but do not expect a quick response. If you write, ensure you provide as much detail as possible.

Ms. Heidrun Weiss
Israelitische Kultusgemeinde Wien,
Matrikelamt, Seitenstettengasse 4, A-1010 Vienna, Austria
Tel: +43 1 531-04172 - Fax: +43 1 533-1577
E-mail: h.weiss@ikg-wien.at
Home page: http://www.ikg-wien.at/

In addition to Vienna, there are the following active Jewish communities in Austria: Graz (Synagogenplatz 1), Innsbruck (Sillgasse 15), Linz (Bethlehemstrasse 26), and Salzburg (Lasserstrasse 8).

Wiener Stadt- und Landesarchiv
The Viennese Jewish Matrikeln have been microfilmed. The microfilms are available in Vienna at the Rathaus (Town Hall) in the Wiener Stadt- und Landesarchiv. The Rathaus archive has long opening hours and is often more convenient than the Israelitische Kultusgemeinde, although the room housing these records is not easy to find. The Rathaus is an enormous complex with tall towers, facing the Ringstrasse. It has three main courtyards, and the entrances are from the two sides, not the front facing the Ringstrasse. It is best to enter the building from the right-hand side (when you look at the building from the Ringstrasse). Then you simply turn right inside the archway and go through the doors marked Stiege 6 (Stairway 6) and start going up the stairs until you reach the floor called '1. Stock' (1st floor). In fact this is not the first floor, it is the third floor, because there is a Parterre and a Zwischengeschoss in between. When you reach this floor you go through the doors, turn left and the first door on your left is the Stadt- und

47

Landesarchiv. Go through the reading room to the glass cubicle at the end and show your passport, saying you want to work on the films of the 'Buecher der israelitischen Kultusgemeinde'. You will be shown into the room behind and left to your own devices. Contact:
Univ.-Prof.Dr.Peter Csendes, Magistrat der Stadt Wien,
Magistratsabteilung 8, Wiener Stadt- und Landesarchiv,
Rathaus, 1082 Wien, Austria
Tel: +43 1 4000-84855 - Fax: +43 1 4000-7238
E-mail: POST@m08.magwien.gv.at.

For civil marriage records (from 1870), birth records (from 1868) and death records (from 1872) of persons who did not belong to a religious community (including many mixed marriages and their children) contact:
Magistrat der Stadt Wien, MA 61 Zivilmatrik, Rathaus, Stiege 8, Patterre, Zimmer 17, C 1, 1010 Wien, Austria. Tel: +43 1 4000-0 (you will be connected)

Vital Statistics (Births, Marriages and Deaths)
Records are only held at local level. Pre-1939 they were held by the parish and now the registers are maintained by Standesant within each Gemeinde (community). Source: Statistics Austria.

Census
Statistics Austria states that no individual census records were retained after the data was collated. The first census was in 1869.

LDS Church FHL - Mormons
The Mormon Church, known as the Church of Jesus Christ of the Latter Day Saints or 'LDS', makes the Vienna Jewish Matrikeln available through its Family History Library (FHL) in Salt Lake City, with branches located throughout the world and open to the public. For most people, this is the most convenient method of researching the Vienna Jewish Matrikeln. Contact your local LDS Library for more information.
See http://www.familysearch.org/Search/searchfhc2.asp to find the FHL nearest to your town. The microfilms are indexed on the FHL Locality Microfiche under 'Austria, Niederoesterreich, Wien - Jewish Records'. If the local FHL does not own copies already, it will order them from Salt Lake City for a very nominal fee. The members of staff are most helpful and one does not need to belong to the Church to use the library. The Church does not proselytise in the library.

The FHL has birth, marriage and death records from the early 19th century to 1895 for the following Jewish communities in the Burgenland: Deutsch Kreuz, Eisenstadt, Frauenkirchen, Gattendorf, Güssing, Kittsee, Kobersdorf, Lackenbach, Rechnitz, St. Pölten and Stadt Schlaining. There are also some civil records between 1895 and 1921 available at the FHL.

A full list of LDS Family History Centres in Great Britain may be seen in the publication entitled *'Jewish Ancestors? A Beginner's Guide to Jewish Genealogy in Great Britain'* - details on page 76. (See pages 11 and 19 for further details.)

CEMETERIES

Cemetery Records

The main Jewish cemeteries in Vienna are located at the Vienna Zentralfriedhof. From 1879 until 1916, the old cemetery, which is located at 1.Gate/I.Tor, was used. From 1917, most burials will be found at 4.Gate/4.Tor. A non-profit organization called 'Schalom' will assist people trying to locate graves in the Jewish cemetery. They have a computerised database of the entire Jewish cemetery. Mag. Walter Pagler is the founder of 'Schalom'. He has an office in a trailer at the First Gate. Mag. Pagler and 'Schalom' are also now looking after other cemeteries in Burgenland, Kärnten, Niederösterreich and Steiermark. They have published a guide (Wegweiser) in German with maps and other information. Mag. Pagler and Schalom can be contacted at:

Verein Schalom
Zentralfriedhof 1 Tor, A1110 Vienna, Austria
Tel/Fax: +43 1 767 1507

The mailing address for the Jewish Cemetery at the Zentralfriedhof is:
Zentralfriedhof 4. Tor, Simmeringer Hauptstrasse 224,
A-1110 Vienna, Austria.

The maps of Zentralfriedhof Cemetery (1/4.Tor) are on the next page.
The maps were kindly supplied by Mag. Walter Pagler of Schalom.

Out of normal opening times, if the cemeteries are locked, keys may be obtained from the Israelitsche Kultusgemeinde Wien (address on page 47) or from the Society 'Schalom' (trailer/office located at the first gate of the cemetery) before an intended visit.

Wein-Waehring Cemetery

This cemetery, used between 1784 and 1879, contains graves of the famous, amongst which are: Arnstein, Biedermann, Herz, Hofmann von Hoffmannstall, Koenigswarter, Laemel, Leidesdorfer, Sichrovsky, Todesco, Wertheimstein etc.

Other Austrian cemeteries

The respective local community offices also have keys, but these may have restricted opening times and are closed on Saturdays, Sundays and holidays. Conditions of these vary considerably. For further details enquire as above.

Zentralfriedhof Cemetery (1 Tor/Gate 1), Vienna

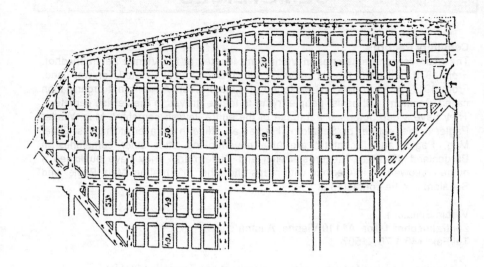

Zentralfriedhof Cemetery (4 Tor/Gate 4), Vienna
ORIENTIERUNGSPLAN NEUER ISRAELITISCHER FRIEDHOF

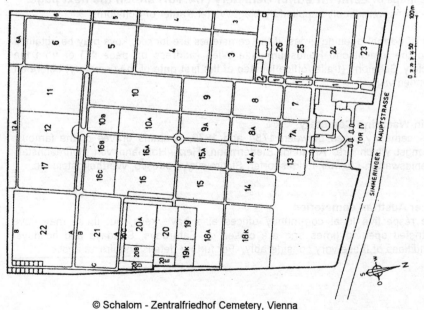

© Schalom - Zentralfriedhof Cemetery, Vienna

OTHER RECORDS AND ADDRESSES

AUSTRIAN NATIONAL LIBRARY

In the Austrian National Library (Österreichische Nationalbibliothek) you can view a number of useful resources. See Web site: http://www.onb.ac.at/. The entrance is from the Heldenplatz in front of the Hofburg palace, opposite the Volksgarten. The Library has a newspaper archive downstairs, where you can view old copies of the Neues Wiener Abendblatt (microfilm 394.205 - D.Per) and the Neue Freie Presse (microfilm 393.929 - D). These are the two papers in which Jewish families always put death notices. (The Neue Freie Presse dating from 1885-January 1939 is available at the British Library - Newspaper Library - see this section on page 12.) The notices usually contain names of all family members (also parents, brothers, sisters, in-laws, etc.). Also in the library you can get Lehmann's Wiener Wohnungsanzeiger (cat. 393.867 - C.Per). This is an alphabetical listing of all heads of household in Vienna fom 1859 onwards. It is like a telephone directory for the 19th century without telephone numbers. The Mormon FHL has these directories available for 1870, 1902, 1906, 1908 and 1925.

DOKUMENTATIONSARCHIV DES ÖSTERREICHISCHEN WIDERSTANDES

The Dokumentationsarchiv (Documentation Archive of the Austrian Resistance) in the Altes Rathaus in Wipplingerstrasse in Vienna is an attempt by the Austrian government to produce something like a memorial (yizkor) book for Austrian Jews murdered in the Holocaust. They have a large archive and library with a lot of information on the Holocaust. They are very helpful.

Dokumentationsarchiv des Österreichischen Widerstandes
Altes Rathaus, Wipplingerstrasse 8, A-1010 Wien, Austria
Tel: +43 1 534-36/01779 - Fax: +43 1 534-36-7171
E-mail: docarch@email.adis.at
Home page: http://www.doew.at

FREMDENKARTEI (Citizenship)

The Wiener Stadt und Landesarchiv (see section - Household Registration Records above) has records of all immigrants to Vienna between 1870 and 1880. The forms are arranged alphabetically. The entries contain names of all members of the family and their exact date of birth, place of origin, occupation, religion, and address in Vienna.

GENEALOGICAL SOCIETIES

Austrian Heraldic-Genealogical Society 'Adler' (Eagle)

The Austrian Heraldic-Genealogical Society 'Adler' was founded in 1870 and maintains a library devoted to genealogy, which includes obituary notices, heraldic crests, seals and periodicals. There is a huge collection of death notices from Vienna newspapers (several bookcases full). As in the USA it was often the custom to list the family members with their relation to the deceased in these notices, and

51

even give their professions. The Society provides information (not by phone) and may be able to connect you with people who can help in your research. When contacting the Society from abroad include international reply coupons. The library is open for visitors (special visitors' fee). BohMor member Georg Gaugusch (georg.gaugusch@aon.at) deals especially with old and ennobled Jewish families, and is very knowledgable in these areas.

Address of the Austrian Heraldic-Genealogical Society Adler (Eagle):
Heraldisch-Genealogische Gesellschaft 'Adler' (Eagle)
Universitaetsstrasse 6, Tuer 10, A-1096 Wien, Austria.
E-mail: society.adler.vienna@chello.at

Bohemian-Moravian Genealogical Society
The purpose of this Special Interest Group is to serve as a clearing-house for genealogical and historical information relating to Jewish communities in the areas formerly known as Bohemia and Moravia. Most of this area is today the Czech Republic. Because of the very close ties between the Bohemia-Moravia area and Austria (especially Vienna, where so many Bohemian and Moravian Jews migrated in the 19th century), discussions also include information related to Austrian Jewish genealogy. Sharing of research resources and advice is the focus of this discussion group. It would also like to gather information about life in Bohemia and Moravia, and make it available on-line to those who are interested. It is collecting information of genealogical and historical interest, including but not limited to photographs, business and residential directories, census lists, property owners' lists, tax rolls, original manuscripts and translations from memorial (yizkor) books.

Web site: http://www.jewishgen.org/BohMor/ (the web site of BohMor SIG, the JewishGen Bohemia-Moravia Special Interest Group)

In addition, you may join the over 270 members of the BohMor SIG by subscribing, free of charge, to: http://www.jewishgen.org/listserv/sigs_add.htm.

HISTORIKERKOMMISSION (Historians' Commission)
The Austrian government has set up a commission to write a series of reports on the Nazi era and its aftermath.

Historikerkommission der Republik Österreich
Nottendorfer Gasse 2, A-1030 Wien, Austria
Tel: +43 1 79540 DW 180 - Fax: +43 1 79540 DW 186
E-mail: hiskom@oesta.gv.at
Home page: http://www.historikerkommission.gv.at

HOLOCAUST VICTIMS' INFORMATION AND SUPPORT CENTRE
In July 1999, the Federation of Jewish Communities in Austria, together with the Committee for Jewish Claims on Austria, the Council of Jews from Austria in Israel and the American Council for Equal Compensation of Nazi Victims from Austria, established the Holocaust Victims' Information and Support Centre (HVISC) for Jewish Holocaust survivors in and from Austria. The HVISC documents individual

cases of Nazi persecution and Holocaust-era assets in order to build a premise for their future restitution or compensation.

The Holocaust Victims' Information and Support Centre is a political body representing Jewish Nazi victims and their heirs. First and foremost, the HVISC seeks to achieve justice for Holocaust survivors finally and without delay. The HVISC does not provide legal representation for Holocaust victims or their heirs nor will it administer restitution funds. Any funds received as restitution or compensation payments will be made available exclusively and directly to Holocaust victims or their heirs. The services of the HVISC are provided free of charge unless otherwise agreed.

Holocaust Victims' Information and Support Centre
Desider Friedmann-Platz 1, A-1010 Vienna, Austria
Tel: +43 1 531 04-201 - Fax: +43 1 531 04-219
E-mail: anlaufstelle@ikg-wien.at

HOUSEHOLD REGISTRATION RECORDS
In Vienna as well as in other cities and countries in Continental Europe it is, even today, mandatory for all residents to register with the police. In Vienna the Wiener Stadt- und Landesarchiv (Magistratsabteilung 8) has registrations up to 1948. The Zentralmeldeamt der Bundespolizeidirektion Wien, 1092 Wien, Rossauerlaende 5 has the registrations after 1948. There may be a fee for a search at these institutions.

The Mormon FHL has a huge collection of Vienna Household Registration Records on microfilm. The films are indexed only on the FHL microfiche under 'Austria, Niederoesterreich, Wien, Population'. (NB: It is not shown in the FHL CD-ROM catalogue or in on-line FamilySearch catalogue.) Described as follows: Title: Polizeiliches Meldeamt. Meldezettel (Household or Population Registration), it covers the period of about 1890-1924. The records are on 2,661 rolls of microfilm. The registration was recorded on individual cards that include names of husband, wife, children, character/occupation, birth date or age, birth place, religion, marital status, current and previous places of residence, and departure date (includes death) and place. The films are listed by male and then female. They are labelled by the first surname (maybe) on the film. The filing order is described on the FHL microfiche (similar to Soundex) but it's not easy to use.

INSTITUTE FOR THE HISTORY OF THE JEWS IN AUSTRIA
This Institute was founded in 1988 and is housed in the former synagogue of St. Poelten, 60 kilometers west of Vienna. Its task is to carry out comprehensive research into the history and culture of the Jews in Austria, from the Middle Ages up to the present day.

Institute for the History of the Jews in Austria
Dr. Karl Renner-Promenade 22, A-3100 St. Pölten
Tel: +43 2742 77171-0 - Fax: +43 2742 77171-15
E-mail: injoest@magnet.at
Home page: http://members.magnet.at/injoest/

KRIEGSARCHIV (War Archives)
The Kriegsarchiv is part of the Staatsarchiv and contains personal details of members of the Imperial armed forces who originated from Vienna and other parts of what is present-day Austria (other files were sent to Budapest and Prague). For ordinary soldiers you have to know date of entry into the armed forces and which regiment, and then you can see the 'Grundbuchblatt'. However, officers are listed in an alphabetically organized archive of so-called 'Qualifikationslisten' (the file numbers are all QUALL ###) and can be accessed by name alone! The files contain mainly military career details, but it is possible to pick out details of date and place of birth, marital status and whether and when children were born.
See: http://german.genealogy.net/gene/reg/AUT/karchiv.html for a detailed description of the archive in German, or contact:

Österreichisches Staatsarchiv
Kriegsarchiv, Nottendorfergasse 2, A-1030 Vienna, Austria
http://www.oesta.gv.at/ebestand/ekv/efr1_kv.htm (see pages 55,56)

MUSEUMS
Jewish Community Centre, Vienna
Seitenstettengasse 4, A-1010, Vienna, Austria.
Most Jewish birth, marriage and death certificates have survived and are the property of the Jewish community of Vienna. There are also records of survivors. Enquiries should be made to the above address.

Jewish Museum, Vienna
Dorotheergasse 11, Vienna, Austria.
Tel: +43 1 535 04 31   Fax: +43 1 535 04 24
Web site: http://www.jmw.at/de/museum.html
First opened in 1993 and after refurbishment re-opened in 1995. It houses the remnants of the collections of the old Jewish Museum of Vienna, which was closed by the Nazis in 1938.

Library of the Jewish Museum, Vienna
(Second Floor) Seitenstettengasse 4, 1010 Vienna, Austria.
Tel: +43 1 535 04 31-82   Fax: +43 1 535 50 46
E-mail: bibliothek@jmw.at
Web site: http://www.jmw.at
Holds large collection of books mainly on the subject of the history of the Jews of Austria and Jewish community of Vienna.

Simon Wiesenthal Documentation Centre
Salztorgasse 6, Vienna, Austria
E-mail: Webmaster@wiesenthal.com
Web site: http://www.wiesenthal.com
International Centre for Holocaust remembrance, the defence of human rights and the Jewish people. The Centre carries on the continuing fight against bigotry and anti-Semitism and pursues an active agenda of related contemporary issues. To visit the Centre an appointment is necessary.

The following two museums do not hold specific genealogical information but do receive and respond to requests from time to time from genealogists:

Sigmund Freud Museum
Berggasse 19, A-1090 Vienna, Austria
Tel: +43 1 319 15 96 - Fax: +43 1 317 02 79
E-mail: freud-museum@t0.or.at
Web site: http://freud.t0.or.at/freud/home-d.htm
Museum is about the life and work of Sigmund Freud, who lived here from 1891-1938.

Arnold Schönberg Centre
Palais Fanto, Schwarzenbergplatz 6, A-1030 Vienna, Austria
Tel: +43 1 712 18 88 - Fax: +43 1 712 18 88 88
E-mail: office@schoenberg.at
Web site: http://www.schoenberg.at

NATIONALFONDS DER REPUBLIK ÖSTERREICH FÜR OPFER DES NATIONALSOZIALISMUS (National fund of the Austrian Republic for victims of Nazism)
The Austrian government has set up a fund to assist needy Holocaust victims from Austria. The main task of the Nationalfonds is to provide financial support for victims of National Socialism as quickly, flexibly and unbureaucratically as possible. It was established in 1995, the 50th Anniversary of the Second Republic, in order to 'remember all the immense wrong inflicted on millions of human beings by Nazism as well as the fact that Austrians, too, were involved in these crimes'. To date, over 18,000 applicants worldwide have received payments from the Nationalfonds. The Fonds pay according to age priority. In case of grave illness or social need, payments to younger persons can be made earlier - in case of social hardship the amount of 70,000 Austrian Schillings (approximately $6,000 US dollars or £3,500) can be tripled.

Contact:
Nationalfonds der Republik Österreich für Opfer
des Nationalsozialismus
Mag. Hannah Lessing, General Secretary
Dr. Karl-Renner-Ring 3 Parlament, 1017 Wien, Austria
Tel: +43 1 408 1263/64 - Fax: +43 1 408 0389
E-mail: nationalfonds@eunet.at
Home page: http://www.nationalfonds.parlament.gv.at

Application for compensation may be made through the Austrian Embassy in London.

ÖESTERREICHISCHES STAATSARCHIV
Dr. Hubert Steiner at the Öesterreichisches Staatsarchiv has produced a search aid for the property lists, to which all Jews in Vienna were forced to register in 1938. The list is also available on the Web at:
http://www.avotaynu.com/HolocaustList/a2.htm. These records are filed by sequence of submission, not by name, so without Dr. Steiner's laudable work it

would be quite impossible to find anything. Now you can e-mail Dr. Steiner and ask him to look up the file number of the person you are searching for, and then request a photocopy of the file from the Staatsarchiv. Dr. Steiner's address is:
Dr. Hubert Steiner, Österreichisches Staatsarchiv
Archiv der Republik, Nottendorfergasse 2, A-1030 Vienna, Austria
E-mail: h.steiner@teleweb.at

The property lists contain details of possessions and property and also sometimes contain data on what happened to the persons concerned, including their exile addresses and so on. Practically all Jews in Vienna in 1938 completed one, because if they didn't everything was confiscated. These records may be valuable to families making claims in the Austrian Bank Holocaust Litigation Class Action, see Web site: http://www.austrianbankclaims.com.

POSTSPARKASSE REPORT
The Austrian Postsparkasse Savings Bank has published a report on assets held by Jewish Austrians that were taken by the Nazis. The entire list of account-holders is available on the web at:
http://www.psk.co.at/pskgruppe/report/index.html.

Contact:
Österreichische Postsparkasse AG, Ref: 'research report'
Georg Coch-Platz 2, A-1010 Vienna, Austria
Fax: +43 1 51400-1700 or 1762
The report itself is written by Prof. Oliver Rathkolb, director of the Bruno Kreisky Institute.

The Bruno Kreisky Archives Foundation
Univ.Doz. D Dr. Oliver Rathkolb
Rechte Wienzeile 97, A-1050 Vienna, Austria
Tel +43 1 545 75 35/32 - Fax +43 1 545 30 97
E-mail: rathkolb@kreisky.vienna.at
Home page: http://members.vienna.at/kreisky

INTERNET

BohMor is developing a site describing the various cities and towns in Austria with Jewish communities - go to Austrian GemeindeView on the BohMor web site at http://www.jewishgen.org/BohMor/ausgmnvw.htm

In addition, see the BohMor Page of Links.at:
http://www.jewishgen.org/BohMor/all_link.html

NAME	WEB SITE
Archives in Austria	http://www.oesta.gv.at/deudiv/arch_oe.htm
Austrian Concentration Camp Victims'	http://www.jewishgen.org/yizkor/austria/ -
Austrian Facts & Figures	http://www.information@austria.org.uk
Austrian GemeindeView	http://www.jewishgen.org/bohmor/gemeinde.htm
Austrian Genealogy Web	http://www.rootsweb.com/~autwgw/
Austrian Jewish Cemeteries	http://www.jewishgen.org/cemetery/austria.htm
Austrian Jewish Museum in Eisenstadt	http://members.magnet.at/oejudmus/
Austrian JewishNet	http://www.jewishnet.at
Austrian National Library	http://www.onb.ac.at/
Austrian Press & Information Service	http://www.austria.org/
Austrian State Archives	http://www.oesta.gv.at/
Avotaynu	http://www.avotaynu.com/
Beginner's Guide to Austrian-Jewish Genealogy	http://www.jewishgen.org/bohmor/ausguide.htm
City of Vienna	http://www.magwien.gv.at
City of Vienna Info on Tracing your Roots	http://www.magwien.gv.at/ma08/ancestors.htm
Cyndi's List of Genealogical Sites on the Internet	http://www.cyndislist.com/
English-German Translation	http://babelfish.altavista.digital.com/
Hamburg Emigration Lists	http://hamburg.de/LinkToYourRoots/english/welcome.htm
Headstone Hunter	http://www.headstonehunter.com/
Institute for Historical Family Research	http://ihff.nwy.at/index.htm
Jewish Community of Vienna	http://www.ikg-wien.at (Israelitische Kultusgemeinde Wien)
Jewish English-German Dictionary	http://www.de.freebsd.org/~wosch/dict/dict.cgi
JewishGen Home page	http://www.jewishgen.org/
JGSGB	http://www.jgsgb.ort.org
Jewish Museum Hohenems	http://www2.vol.at/jmh/
Jewish Museum of Vienna	http://www.jmw.at/
Jewish News	http://www.hagalil.com/austria/index.htm
Mauthausen Memorial	http://www.mauthausen-memorial.gv.at/index.html
Old German Script - Learn how to read it!	http://www2.genealogy.net/gene/misc/scripts.html
Republic of Austria homepage	http://www.austria.gv.at/e
Tracing Your Ancestors in Vienna	http://www.magwien.gv.at/ma08/ancestors.htm
U.S. Holocaust Memorial Museum	http://www.ushmm.org/

PART III
GENERAL INFORMATION

BIBLIOGRAPHY

Stammbaum

The German-Jewish genealogical journal 'Stammbaum' (family tree) is published twice a year by the Leo Baeck Institute in New York. Although 'Stammbaum' focuses on Germany, the scope includes Alsace, Austria, Bohemia, Switzerland and other areas with linguistic and historic relevance. (The Jewish Genealogical Society of Great Britain subscribes to it and the library has a complete set.) A list of archivists associated with Jewish archives and collections was published in Issue 8-9 (July 1996). Web site: http://www.jewishgen.org/stammbaum/

Avotaynu

The American-Jewish genealogical journal 'Avotaynu' is published four times a year, and contains some articles about German-Jewish genealogy. (The Jewish Genealogical Society of Great Britain has a subscription to it and a complete set is kept in the library.) Web site: http://www.avotaynu.com

NB: Where known, the whereabouts of a book has been indicated by a symbol for the Library concerned thus:

BL	British Library
JC	Jews' College Library (London School of Jewish Studies)
JGSGB	Jewish Genealogical Society's Library at Kinloss Gardens, London, N.3.
	(For use by JGSGB Society members only)
STN	Southampton University – Parkes Library
UCL	University College London, Jewish Studies Library
WL	Wiener Library, London, W.1.

GENERAL

Blumenau, Ralph
> A History of the Jews in German-Speaking Lands. University of the Third Age, London, 1995 **(JC)**

Ellmann-Krüger, Angelika
> Library Resources for German Jewish Genealogy **(JGSGB)**

Freund, Ismar
> Die Emanzipation der Juden in Preussen (Emancipation of Prussian Jews) **(UCL)**

Gillman, Peter and Leni
> Collar the Lot! Quartet Books, London, 1980. (Describes the internment of German and Austrian Jewish refugees on the Isle of Man, in Canada and Australia in 1940-41 on Churchill's orders) **(UCL)**

Niewyk, Donald L
The Jews in Weimar Germany. Manchester University Press, 1980. (Covers the history of the Jews in Germany from 1918-1933) **(JC UCL)**

Reichsbund Jüdischer Frontsoldaten
Die Jüdischen Gefallenen des deutschen Heeres, der deutschen Marine und der deutschen Schutztruppen 1914-1918. (Lists of Jewish members of the German Forces killed in World War I. It gives names, place of residence, date and place of birth and date of death) 1932 **(BL)**

Ribbe, Wolfgang and Henning, Eckart
Taschenbuch für Familiengeschichtsforschung (Pocket book for genealogical research.) Gives addresses of German archives including private archives kept by rulers of former independent territories. Neustadt a.d. Aisch 1995

Towey, Peter
An Introduction to Tracing your German Ancestors. Federation of Family History Societies, 1998. Very useful book

Verdenhalven, Fritz
Die deutsche Schrift: The German Script, Ein Übungsbuch. Degener, Neustadt an der Aisch: 1991. Bi-lingual. This is invaluable for teaching yourself to read German script

Handbuch des Jüdischen Wissens, 1935 (small Jewish encyclopaedia). Philo-Lexicon

The following 6 entries are from the Statistisches Bundesamt in Wiesbaden and will be available for viewing in the JGSGB Library:

Kirchliche Verhältnisse: Jüdische Gemeinden in Deutschland (Churches: Jewish communities in Germany) for the years 1950, 1960, 1970, 1980, 1990 and 1992 until 1998. (Source: Statistisches Bundesamt, Statistisches Jahrbuch, 1952, 1961, 1971, 1994 and 1999)

Die Religionsgliederung der Bevölkerung des Deutschen Reichs (Religious affiliation of the population of the German Reich), 1939, pp 173-176, and Sonderbeilage zu 'Wirtschaft und Statistik' (Special attachment to Economy and Statistics) relating to the population census of 17 May 1939, pp. 1-15. (Source: Wirtschaft und Statistik, 1st May edition, 1941, 21st year, No. 9 published by Statistisches Reichsamt on 20 May 1941)

Die Bevölkerung des Deutschen Reichs nach den Ergebnissen der Volkszählung von 1933 (The population of the German Reich based on the results of the 1933 population census) No. 5, Die Glaubensjuden im Deutschen Reich (Confessing Jews in the German Reich), pp 5/7 - 5/30. (Source: Statistik des Deutschen Reichs, Vol. 451, 5 - Berlin, 1936)

Juden in der DDR (Jews in the GDR), pp. 1192-1203 (Source: Deutschland Archiv, 11/86)

Die Glaubensjuden im Deutschen Reich (Confessing Jews in the German Reich), pp 5/5 - 5/9 and 5/24. (Source: Statistik des Deutschen Reichs, Vol.451)

Die demographische Entwicklung der Juden in Deutschland von der Mitte des 19. Jahrhunderts bis 1933 (Demographic evolution of Jews in Germany from the mid-

BERLIN

Bendt, Veronica

Synagogen unter dem Nationalsozialismus. Synagogen in Berlin (Synagogues in Berlin). 2 volumes, 1983. Contains many photographs

Geiger, Ludwig

Geschichte der Juden in Berlin (The history of Jews in Berlin) **(UCL)**

Melcher, Peter

Weissensee. Ein Friedhof als Spiegelbild Jüdischer Geschichte in Berlin. (A cemetery as mirror of Jewish history in Berlin) 1987. Contains many photographs **(JC JGSGB)**

Roth, Andrew and Frajman, Michael

The Gold Apple Guide to Jewish Berlin. 1998

(Various Authors)

Wegweiser durch das jüdische Berlin (Guide through Jewish Berlin). Nicolai. 1987

Juden in Berlin 1671 - 1945. (Jews in Berlin 1671-1945). Nicolai. 1988

Jüdisches Adressbuch für Gross-Berlin:Ausgabe 1931 (reprinted in 1994 by Arani-Verlag, Berlin). It is like a telephone book for Jews who lived in Berlin **(WL)**

BAVARIA

Aretin, J von

Geschichte der Juden in Bayern (History of Bavarian Jews) 1803 **(BL JC)**

Ballin, Grete

Geschichte der Juden in Fürth 1578-1943 (History of Jews in Fürth 1578-1943)

Bamberger, Naphtalie

Geschichte der Juden von Kitzingen. Festgabe anlaesslich des 25 Jaehrigen Bestehens der Synagoge Kitzingen (1883 -1908). (History of Jews of Kitzingen issued on the occasion of 25th anniversary of the Synagogue in Kitzingen)

Brandt, Harm-Hinrich

Hundert Jahre Kitzinger Synagogue. Zur Geschichte des Judentums in Mainfranken. Mainfrankische Hefte, Heft 81. (100 years of Synagogue in Kitzingen. Addition to the history of Jews in Lower Franconia)

Brandt, Harm-Hinrich

Zwischen Schutzherrschaft und Emanzipation. Mainfränkische Studien. Band 39. (Between protectorate and emancipation)

Fuchs, E.M

Uber die ersten Niederlassungen der Juden in Mittelfranken (First settlement of Jews in Middle Franconia)

Michel, Thomas

Die Juden in Gaukönigshofen/Unterfranken 1550 - 1924 (Jews in Gaukönigshofen/Lower Franconia 1550-1924) **(BL)**

Mönchhoff, Ursula
Jüdische Schüler des Gymnasiums Fridericianum Erlangen 1815 - 1861 Erlanger Bausteine zur fränkischen   Heimatkunde. (Jewish pupils in the Gymnasium Fridericianum Erlangen 1815-1861)

Ophir, Baruch Zvi
Pinkas Ha-Kehillot – Germany Vol. 1: Bavaria 1972 **(JC STN)**

Ophir, Baruch Zvi
Die jüdischen Gemeinden in Bayern 1918 - 1945 1979 **(BL WL)**

Rockenmaier, Dieter W
Buchfuhrung des Todes. Die Endlosung der Judenfrage im damaligen Gau Mainfranken. (Bookkeeping of death - the final solution of the Jewish question in the former region Lower Franconia)

Schwarz, Stefan
Die Juden in Bayern im Wandel der Zeiten (Bavarian Jews in changing times)

Schwierz, Israel
Steinerne Zeugnisse Jüdischen Lebens in Bayern (Book giving details on former Jewish Communities in Bavaria, locations of their synagogues, schools, cemeteries etc) **(UCL)**

Strätz, Reiner
Biographisches Handbuch Würzburger Juden 1900 - 1945 (Very good book giving details of all Jews known to have lived in Würzburg during 1900-1945) **(BL)**

OTHER PARTS OF GERMANY:
STETTIN
Ambrose, Kenneth
The Suitcase in the Garage (History of a family of Stettin Jews) 1996 **(JGSGB)**

Peiser, Jacob
Geschichte der Synagogengemeinde zu Stettin (History of the Stettin Community) 1965 **(UCL)**

Rosenfeld, Else and Luckner, Gertrud
Lebenszeichen aus Piaski (Letters from Stettin Jews from their deportation to the Polish village of Piaski nr. Lublin) 1968 **(UCL)**

FOR FORMER PROVINCE OF POSEN/POZNAN
Barty
Grand Duchy of Posen (Poznan) under Prussian Rule. Changes in the economic position of the Jewish population 1815-1848. (Leo Baeck Institute Year Book XVII)

Bergmann, Eugen von
Zur Geschichte der Entwicklung deutscher, polnischer und jüdischer Bevölkerung der Provinz Posen (Poznan) seit 1824. (History of the development of German, Polish and Jewish population of the province Posen (Poznan) since 1824)

Breslauer, Bernhard
Die Abwanderung der Juden aus der Provinz Posen (Poznan) 1912.
(The emigration of Jews from the province Posen (Poznan))

Heppner A & Herzberg J
Aus der Vergangenheit und Gegenwart der Juden und der jüdischen Gemeinden in
den Posener Landen 1904 - 1913. (Of past and present times of Jews and Jewish
communities in the Posen (Poznan) regions) 1921-1929) **(UCL)**

Hirschberg, Isidor
Verzeichnis sämtlicher Naturalisierter Israeliten im Grossherzogtum Posen
(Poznan). (Lists of all naturalised Jews in the Grand Duchy of Posen (Poznan).)
Published: Bromberg 1836. The Bundesarchiv and the Leo Baeck Institute have
copies of this rare document)

Jacob Jacobson Collection (Leo Baeck Institute)
Ortsregister sämtlicher naturalisierter Israeliten in Grossherzogtum Posen (Poznan)
1830. (Local register of all naturalised Jews in the Grand Duchy of Posen (Poznan)
1830)

Luft, Edward
Naturalized Jews of Grand Duchy of Posen (Poznan) 1834/35. (Published recently
in English) **(JC)**

Reineke, A
Quellen zur Geschichte der Juden in den Archiven der neuen   Bundesländer, vol.1
(Sources for the history of the Jews in the archives of the former East Germany)
(JGSGB)

Zarchin, Michael
Juden in der Provinz Posen (Poznan) - (Jews in the province Posen (Poznan)) **(JC)**

MORAVIA
Gold, Hugo (publisher)
Die Juden und Judengemeinden Mährens in Vergangenheit und Gegenwart.
Published 1929 (Moravian Jews and Jewish Communities in the past and present)

AUSTRIA
Berkley, G
Vienna and its Jews 1988 - with index **(UCL)**

Fraenkel, Josef
The Jews of Austria: essays on their life. Published in London 1967 **(JC UCL)**

Gold, Hugo
Geschichte der Juden in Österreich: ein Gedenkbuch (History of the Jews in
Austria: a memorial book). Tel Aviv: Olamenu, 1971 **(JC UCL WL)**

Gold, Hugo
Geschichte der Juden in Wien; ein Gedenkbuch. (History of Jews in Vienna: a
memorial book) Tel Aviv, Olamenu, 1966 **(JC UCL WL)**

Gold, Hugo
Österreichische Juden in der Welt: ein bio-bibliographisches Lexikon (Austrian Jews in the World: a bibliographical dictionary), Hugo Gold. 1971 **(JC UCL WL)**

Gold, Hugo
Untergegangenen Judengemeinden des Gedenkbuchs des Burgenlandes 1971 **(JC)**

Grunwald, Max
Geschichte der Juden in Wien, 1625-1740 (History of Jews in Vienna, 1625-1740) 1913

Grunwald, Max
Geschichte der Wiener Juden bis 1914, der Schuljugend erzählt. Im Anschlusse an die Jahrhundertfeier des Tempels der Inneren Stadt gewidmet vom Vorstande der Israelitischen Kultusgemeinde Wien. (History of Viennese Jews until 1914 for the school youth. On the occasion of the hundredth anniversary celebration of the inner city temple, dedicated by the Board of the Jewish community in Vienna) **(UCL)**

Grunwald, Max
Samuel Oppenheimer und sein Kreis (ein Kapitel aus der Finanzgeschichte Österreichs) (Samuel Oppenheimer and his circle (a chapter from the financial history of Austria) **(UCL)**

Grunwald, Max
Vienna

Senekovic, Dagmar
Handy guide to Austrian Genealogical Records. 1979

HOLOCAUST

Bernadac, C
Dachau. Train 7909: Destination Dachau **(WL)**

Debski, J
Auschwitz Death Books for Auschwitz. Remnants.1995. Vol 1: Chronology; Biography. SS Men.Vol 2: names A-L Vol 3: names M-Z **(WL)**

Gilbert, Martin
Atlas of the Holocaust. 1982 **(JGSGB)**

Oppenheim, A
The Chosen People. Story of 222 transport. Bergen-Belsen to Palestine **(WL)**

Germany Gedenkbuch: Opfer der Verfolgung der deutschen Juden. 1986 2 Vols Lists over 128000 Jews who died in the Holocaust **(WL)**

ENGLAND
Specht, Maureen
The German Hospital in London and the Community it served 1845-1948

GERMAN LANGUAGE, TRANSLATIONS AND SCRIPT

Bentz, Edna M
Decipher German Records. Published by the author San Diego Ca. 1993.
A book for fellow genealogists, giving many variants of letter formation and lists of specialised vocabulary for occupations, cause of death etc

Naumann, Horst
Dictionary of German Names

Shea, Jonathan D and Hofman, William F
Following the paper trail (JGSGB)

Verdenhalven, Fritz
Die Deutsche Schrift: The German Script, Ein Übungsbuch. Degener, Neustadt an der Aisch: 1991. Bi-lingual. Invaluable to teach yourself to read German Script (see page 69)

Journal at the London School of Jewish Studies (Jews College) Library
Jüdische Familien Forschung (Jewish Family Research). 1924-1938, 50 issues bound in one volume. Journal of the first Jewish Genealogical Society.

BOOKS IN WIENER LIBRARY
Cemeteries - Germany

Harpstedt	The Harpstedt Jewish Cemetery Jolles, M 1966
Hohenlimburg	Der jüdische Friedhof in Hohenlimburg. Includes Kirchhofsregister der Israelitischen Gemeinde zu Hohenlimburg. Böning, 1986. (The Jewish cemetery in Hohenlimburg. Includes the register of the cemetery of the Jewish community of Hohenlimburg)
Jebenhausen	Memor Buch: Die jüdischen Friedhöfe Jebenhausen und Göppingen. (Memorial Book: Jewish cemeteries in Jebenhausen and Göppingen) Bamberger, N 1990
Lippstadt	Der jüdische Friedhof in Lippstadt. (The Jewish cemetery in Lippstadt) Fennenkoter, H 1989
Lubeck	Über Zeit und Ewigkeit. Die jüdischen Friedhöfe in Mosling und Lubeck. (About time and eternity. The Jewish cemeteries in Moslin and Lubeck) Schreiber, A 1998
Schwelm	Hebräische Inschriften auf dem jüdischen Friedhof in Schwelm. (Hebrew inscriptions in the Jewish cemetery in Schwelm)

Siegen-Wittgenstein	Die jüdischen Friedhöfe im Kreis Siegen-Wittgenstein. (Jewish cemeteries in the district Siegen-Wittgenstein) Dietermann, K 1991
Soest	Der jüdische Friedhof in Soest. 1993
Sulzburg	Der jüdische Friedhof in Sulzburg. Kahout, J 1990
Wesel	Nur Gräber bleiben mir. Jüdische Friedhöfe in Wesel. (All I am left with is graves. Jewish cemeteries in Wesel) Brocke, M 1988
Württemberg	Jüdische Gotteshäuser und Friedhöfe. (Jewish synagogues and cemeteries) 1932

Lists at Wiener Library

List of displaced German scholars 1935-9

List of Jewish Lawyers at the Reichsgericht (German Supreme Court)

Newspapers at Wiener Library

Jüdische Rundschau - 1917 onwards - not complete

Aufbau (NewYork) - 1945 onwards

Berliner Tageblatt - 1925 to 1938

Illustrierte Neue Welt - Vienna (founded T. Herzl 1897) odd copies

Gemeindeblatt, Hamburg 1933 , Berlin 1936.

Die jüdische Presse Berlin - 1870 to 1934

ABOUT *SHEMOT*
Shemot is the Journal of The Jewish Genealogical Society of Great Britain.

It is published quarterly and is free to members of the Society. Individual copies of any issue of *Shemot* may be purchased from:

The Jewish Genealogical Society of Great Britain
PO Box 13288, LONDON, N3 3WD.
E-mail: jgsgb@ort.org
Web site: www.jgsgb.ort.org

If you are trying to trace *Shemot* in a public library, it may help to quote the international reference number ISSN 0969-2258.

Shemot contains articles of a genealogical nature, which range from the personal experiences of an individual member including research methods and sources used to papers on specific areas of research.

USEFUL ARTICLES
The JGSGB Web site contains a complete list of articles. The following resources are articles written in *Shemot* in connection with German and Austrian research and may be of assistance in researching your families.

Year	Month	Vol	No	Subject/Author
1995	February	3	1	Research in Hamburg *by Jacqueline Gill*
				The Jews of Northern Bavaria *by Thea Skyte*
	October	3	3	Holocaust Project for AJGS
	December	3	4	A Journey Back in Time by *Hazel Swerdlow & Harold Hodes*
1996	July	4	2	Holocaust Victims and the IGI *by John Levy*
	October	4	3	Yad Vashem's Web Site Changes
1997	December	5	4	Living History by *Sylvia Budd*
1999	March	7	1	Local Alien Registers *by John Illingworth*
	June	7	2	The Holocaust & English Jews *by Peter Landé*
	September	7	3	The Jewish Cemetery in Munich *by Alec Shapiro*
	December	7	4	The Wiener Library *by Dr. Cyril Fox*
				Enemy Aliens not Interned *by Lutz Noack*
2000	March	8	1	Making Use of a Yizkor Book *by David Fielker*
				Yizkor Books *by Dr. Cyril Fox & Dr. Saul Issroff*
				A Yizkor Book at the British Library by *Sylvia Budd*
2000	December	8	4	Mid-19th Century Immigration Records at Kew *by Petra Laidlaw*
				The Genealogical Value of Yizkor Books *by Dr. Cyril Fox*

GERMAN TERMS

The following terminology may be of help to you when writing letters or looking at records:

ENGLISH	GERMAN	ENGLISH	GERMAN	ENGLISH	GERMAN
Monday	Montag	January	Januar/*Jänner	August	August
Tuesday	Dienstag	February	Februar	September	September
Wednesday	Mittwoch	March	März	October	Oktober
Thursday	Donnerstag	April	April	November	November
Friday	Freitag	May	Mai	December	Dezember
Saturday	Sonnabend or Samstag	June	Juni		
Sunday	Sonntag	July	Juli		

*Austrian

ENGLISH	GERMAN
Grand-parents	Grosseltern
Grand-mother	Grossmutter
Grand-father	Grossvater
Grand-son	Enkel
Grand-daughter	Enkelin
Son	Sohn
Son-in-law	Schwiegersohn
Daughter	Tochter
Daughter-in-law	Schwiegertochter
Brother	Bruder
Brother-in-law	Schwager
Sister	Schwester
Sister-in-law	Schwägerin
Mother	Mutter
Mother-in-law	Schwiegermutter
Father	Vater
Father-in-law	Schwiegervater
Child	Kind
Marriage	Heirat
Surname	Familienname
Maiden name	Mädchenname
Nee	Geborene (geb.)
Divorce	Scheidung
Cemetery	Friedhof

ENGLISH	GERMAN
Day of Death	Todestag
Died	Gestorben (gest.)
Born	Geboren (geb.)
Birthday	Geburtstag
Synagogue	Synagoge
Inheritance	Erbschaft
Dowry	Mitgift
Trousseau	Ausstattung

OTHER USEFUL TERMS

ENGLISH	GERMAN
Town, City	Stadt
Town Hall	Rathaus
Federal Archive	Bundesarchiv
Town or City archive	Stadtarchiv
State or area (Land) archive	Staatsarchiv
Village Archive	Gemeindearchiv
Census	Volkszählung
Files	Akten
Record (paper) e.g. record of birth, marriage or death	Bestand (plural Bestände)
Pages (e.g when paying for photocopies)	Seiten
A small piece of paper i.e. the slip one fills out when requesting documents	Zettel
Library reference number of 'shelf mark' (**not the space for your signature**)	Signatur
User (this is where one's name goes, **'Unterschrift' means signature)**	Benutzer
Annual town directories (like British street directories, listing inhabitants and businesses)	Adressbuch
Card index, but can be a registration card as well	Kartei
Registration to use the archive, also when inhabitants were registered by the Town Authorities (Einwohnermeldeamt)	Anmeldung
An appointment e.g. to see an archivist	Termin

GERMAN SCRIPT ALPHABET

Older books, newspapers and documents used to be printed in German (Gothic) script, which is no longer used in Germany. There is a manuscript version (used in old handwritten documents) that is virtually impossible to read, unless one has learnt it. Neither has been taught in German schools since World War II.

LOWER CASE		UPPER CASE	
a	a	ℤ	A
b	b	ℬ	B
c	c	ℭ	C
d	d	℗	D
e	e	ℰ	E
f	f	ℱ	F
g	g	℮	G
h	h	ℌ	H
ℐ	i	ℑ	I
i	j	ℑ	J
k	k	ℛ	K
l	l	ℒ	L
m	m	ℳ	M
n	n	ℜ	N
o	o	ℴ	O
p	p	℗	P
q	q	ℴ	Q
r	r	ℜ	R
ſ	s	ℭ	S
t	t	ℑ	T
u	u	ℐ	U
v	v	ℬ	V
w	w	ℬ	W
x	x	ℋ	X
y	y	ℬ	Y
z	z	ℬ	Z
ä	ä	ℤ̈	Ä
ö	ö	ℴ̈	Ö
ü	ü	ℐ̈	Ü
ß	ss		

STANDARD LETTER AND PHRASES

When writing to Germany, it is very important that letters are sent with the correct address. Since the privatisation of the German postal system, letters without an absolutely correct address, zip-code, street number etc., are often returned to sender. There is a publication entitled *Postleitzahlenbuch* (postcode book), which gives all the postcodes. However, the postcodes were changed in 1993 so ensure you do not use postcodes prior to that year.

The following standard letter was taken from the following Web sites:
http://web.inter.nl.net/users/DJGH/letter/textenglish.htm
http://web.inter.nl.net/users/DJGH/letter/textgerman.html.

Dear Sir/Madam,

As a descendant of (name), (born/married/deceased) on (date) in (place), at the time living in (street name), I would like to obtain a copy of (his/her birth/marriage/death certificate).

Enclosed, please find a cheque/money order for the sum of ....

Thank you.

GERMAN EQUIVALENT

Sehr geehrte Herren und Damen,

Als Nachfahre von (name), geboren/verheiratet/verstorben am (date) in (place), damals in (street) lebend, würde ich gerne eine Kopie seiner/ihrer Geburtsurkunde/Heiratsurkunde/Sterbeurkunde erhalten.

Beiliegend entnehmen Sie bitte einen Scheck/Zahlungsanweisung über (amount).

Mit bestem Dank.

ENGLISH	GERMAN
Dear Sir/Madam	Sehr geehrte Herren und Damen
I am trying to trace my family who came from (enter location).	Ich versuche, meine Familie ausfindig zu machen, die in (enter location) ansässig war.
My (enter) lived at the following address in (enter date).	Mein(e) (enter) war (enter date) wohnhaft in (enter address)
I enclose, herewith, details of my (enter name of relative).	Diesem Schreiben füge ich Einzelheiten über meine(n) (relative),...(name) bei.

70

ENGLISH	GERMAN
Please could you send me a copy of the birth certificate for (enter name) born (enter date and place of birth). Please invoice me accordingly.	Könnten Sie mir bitte eine Kopie der Geburtsurkunde senden von (name), geboren am (date) in (location). Bitte schicken Sie mir die Rechnung über etwaige Kosten.
Please could you send me a copy of the marriage certificate for (enter name) married (enter date and place of marriage). Please invoice me accordingly.	Könnten Sie mir bitte eine Kopie der Heiratsurkunde senden von (name), verheiratet am (date) in (location). Bitte schicken Sie mir die Rechnung über etwaige Kosten.
Please could you send me a copy of the death certificate for (enter name) who died (enter date and place of death). Please invoice me accordingly.	Könnten Sie mir bitte eine Kopie der Sterbeurkunde senden von (name), gestorben am (date) in (location.) Bitte schicken Sie mir die Rechnung über etwaige Kosten.
I would be grateful if you could suggest a contact in your town/city/area for locating Jewish records.	Könnten Sie mir bitte jemanden in Ihrer Stadt/Gegend empfehlen der jüdische Dokumente erforschen kann?
I would like to visit your archives/record office, please could you tell me the hours of opening?	Ich möchte gern Ihre Archive/Ihr Standesamt besuchen, Könnten Sie mir bitte die Öffnungszeiten mitteilen?
Do I need to provide identity? (passport)	Brauche ich einen Ausweis oder Reisepass?
How much do you charge for (enter details)?	Wieviel berechnen Sie für (details)?
Please could you tell me how I obtain access/or whom I contact to visit (name) cemetery.	Können Sie mir bitte sagen, wie ich Zugang zum (name) Friedhof bekomme oder an wen ich mich wenden kann den Friedhof zu besuchen?
Please could you send me a list of researchers in your area who are fluent in English.	Könnten Sie mir bitte Namen von Familienforschern, die fliessend English sprechen, senden.
Please could you send me a copy of your town/city map showing your location (and details of public transport).	Bitte schicken Sie mir Ihren Stadtplan mit Angabe Ihrer Adresse und geben Sie mir Hinweise auf öffentliche Verkehrsmittel.
I enclose International coupons to cover the cost of your reply.	Ich füge Internationale Antwortscheine zur Kostendeckung Ihrer Antwort bei.
I would like to thank you in advance for any help you are able to give and I look forward to hearing from you in due course.	Ich möchte Ihnen schon im Voraus für Ihre Hilfe danken und sehe Ihrer Antwort erwartungsvoll entgegen.

INDEX

OTHER GUIDES IN THIS SERIES

Jewish Ancestors?
A Beginner's Guide to Jewish Genealogy in Great Britain
ISBN: 0-9537669-0-X
Edited by Rosemary Wenzerul

NEARING 2000 COPIES SOLD

◆An insight into the world of Jewish genealogy◆
◆A must for the beginner to genealogy◆
◆Packed from cover to cover with useful information◆
◆An inspiration to continue research once started◆

Price: £4.50 (UK) and £6.00/US$10 (overseas)

Jewish Ancestors?
A Guide to Jewish Genealogy in Latvia & Estonia
ISBN: 0-9537669-2-6
Edited by
Arlene Beare and Rosemary Wenzerul
(To be published in March 2001)
◆ Points you in the right direction for researching your
roots in both the UK and in Latvia & Estonia◆
◆An insight into a host of available records◆
◆Useful tips and information for the genealogical traveller to this area◆

Price: £4.50 (UK) and £6.00/US$10 (overseas)

◆UK GUIDE OBTAINABLE FROM◆

The Public Record Office; Family Record Centre; Society of Genealogists; Federation of Family History Societies; S&N Genealogy Supplies Salisbury; Family Tree Magazine Postal Book Service; Guildhall Library Bookshop; The Family History Shop Norwich; Manor House Books; Waterstone's Bookshop Watford; Jewish Museum; London Museum of Jewish Life; Love & Kisses Radlett.

AND ALL GOOD BOOK SHOPS

◆BY POST FROM◆
The Membership Secretary
The Jewish Genealogical Society of Great Britain
PO Box 27061, London N2 OGT
Payment with orders please